From the Other Side
Pourings from the mind of a Bartender

Trixie Tamerlane

Order this book online at www.trafford.com
or email orders@trafford.com

Most Trafford titles are also available at major online book retailers.

Printed in the United States of America.

ISBN: 978-1-4269-5594-5 (sc)
ISBN: 978-1-4269-5595-2 (e)

Trafford rev. 01/14/2010

 www.trafford.com

North America & international
toll-free: 1 888 232 4444 (USA & Canada)
phone: 250 383 6864 ♦ fax: 812 355 4082

This book is for my Reesa...Because nothing
I have ever done has been misunderstood in
Her eyes. Thank you for always believing
In me. Oh...and scoot over 'cause it's
Five thirty...

Introduction

Allow me to introduce myself. I am your local Bartender. Like many of my colorful colleagues, this has been my profession for over a decade. While it is extremely lucrative and entertaining, it is also indescribably annoying. And that my friends, is solely because of *you*. I like to refer to you as the "others". The patrons. The customers. You know… the nuisances. This collection of thoughts and stories is sort of a handbook for you. A go-to guide for what that garbled look on my face might convey. For the other "others", it might come as a wakeup call, or what *not* to do…

Throughout this account of idiocracy, you might find yourself laughing, as you can totally envision the situation, having witnessed a similar event, or having acted as an accompanying party to an alcohol induced debacle. On the other hand, you might find that the majority of consumers (alcohol consumers that is) are completely oblivious to the world *within* the world, altogether ignoring the ones who are serving up their good times with and almost unwavering tolerance for stupidity…notice, I said *almost*.

While most of you are getting up early, to trek through a day that is no doubt synonymous with the previous one, we bartenders are sleeping off an adventure. A night of shots, fights, laughs, and foolishness. While you are battling rush hour, deadlines, and *the man*, we are rousing from a vodka generated coma…only to prepare for yet another night of mayhem. Our job is not an easy one, but every night we stroll behind the bar, ready to create cocktails on demand, ready to face the unpredictable ten hour night that awaits. We do this with a style and grace indigenous to the seasoned mixologist, an ego unparalleled by those of *other* professions, and the knowledge that we can do whatever the hell we want to…because…well, we are closer to the alcohol than you are.

Chapter One
INTOXICOLOGY 101

"When going to a bar….."

When going to a bar, it is imperative to keep a few things in mind, simply to ensure the maximum amount of fun on your evening out. Here are the most important of said things. TIP YOUR BARTENDER. It doesn't matter if it is a two dollar beer or and eight dollar shot. If the bartenders' first impression of you is the guy who doesn't tip…your night is over buddy. You will wait twenty minutes for your next beverage, even if there is no one else standing at the bar. *Trust me*, we will find something to do, just to make you miserable. Remember, I want to wait on you, you pay my cable bill, but, if I am exerting all of this energy to entertain you and your friends, you'd better be letting me know it's appreciated. I can't tell you how many times I have looked past the four people waiting, just to grab the guy who slipped me a twenty on his first round. I am pouring him stronger drinks, paying more attention to him, making sure he has a great night; All the while, he is looking extra cool for having an 'in' with the bartender, plus, he doesn't have to wait to get drinks for his friends. See how it works? You know that saying *'you scratch my back and I will scratch yours'* was actually created by a bartender? Seriously…look it up. Now, the *other* guy, who ordered three rounds of beers and shots and didn't leave me a penny, well, let me just paint a picture of that guys fate for you…

Guy leaning across the bar, empty bottle in hand, signaling the bartender.
Guy: "Excuse me!"
Bartender glances over, laughs, and continues shaking shots for the aforementioned tipper.
Bartender: "Hey, those are on me babe."
Tipper: "Sweet, thanks. Here take one for yourself."
Bartender: "Cheers."
Tipper: "Cheers."
Bartender clinks glasses with Tipper, downs her shot, high fives the group, collects the glasses and turns her back on Guy.
Guy: "Uh, Excuse me...?"
Bartender repeats above scenario three more times with other Tippers and walks by Guy each time, holding up her index finger insinuating that his time will come...eventually.

Now, upon understanding the predicament that he has placed himself in, Guy has one of two options... Even though his ego might be slightly bruised, he can choose to now slide a substantial tip across the bar after every single round, and, with any luck, change his standings with his scorned server of spirits, *or*, he can collect his friends, toss out a derogatory comment before departing, and hopefully seek out another establishment prior to last call. This is the less appealing option for the group that Guy has brought out to party, and the majority of the time, one or more of the friends is slipping a few bucks across the bar in effort to apologize for the dick behavior that we have endured from their so called 'friend.' No doubt, they are accustomed to this sort of rudeness when attempting to hang with this particular pal, which is the reason for the added compensation on their buddies' behalf. The funniest part for us on the other side is, even if he would have tipped a dollar, it would have been a tip, and while he might not have gotten shots bought for him, he wouldn't have been lumped into the category of the Non-Tippers. When will they learn...

I can't quite place my finger on the quarter tippers either. I hand you a dollar fifty in change and you pick up *all* of it, except that one little quarter. It's like you are either stupid, or are deliberately trying to insult my service, by leaving me as little as you possibly can without *not* tipping at all. Well, friend, either way, it is opening up a spot for you on my shit list. That sudden pain in the back of your skull? That's your quarter, I just flicked it at the back of your head. Leave me a bill and stop wasting my time, dickhead.

The second most important stop on your *When going to a bar* itinerary is Patience. Please take into consideration that you are not the **only** one in the bar. That by far is my most hated of violations by the others. Do you yell at the Captain, when he says there will be a delay, due to maintenance? No. Why? Because you want to make sure that your ass gets in the air in one *non* smoldering piece, right? Do you yell at your mom when she is taking forever to mash the potatoes that will be on the table for dinner? No. Why? 'Cause she would smack the shit out of you, and most likely tell you that you can't have any of the potatoes. Do you yell at the old lady in front of you in line at the grocery store? Nope. Why? Because that would just be *rude*. We demand the same courtesy. There are maybe three, sometimes four bartenders on, depending on the size of the joint, and two hundred or more screaming, drunk idiots all lobbying for attention at the same time. While we pride ourselves on being able to hustle, and bang out a few thousand dollars worth of drinks a night, we aren't superhero's, if we were, we could kill you on the spot with bolts of vodka from our eyes. I bet that would do a little more damage than the old lady whacking you with her purse. Contrary to popular belief, there is hardly ever a time after three o'clock that you can walk into a bar and be the only thirsty fella in the joint. With happy hour in full swing, people are coming out of the woodwork, and chances are, your bartender is already about to punch someone. So chill out, wait your turn, and for the love of God, don't tap your fucking glass on the bar.

While I am on the subject of you thinking that you are the only ones in the bar, let me scoot ahead to the end of the night. A simple glance around the room can confirm the notion that there are quite a few *others* standing at the bar, trying to close out their tabs and collect their credit cards before escorting out a one night stand *or* getting behind the wheel, - both of which, by the way are *excellent* ideas- so please, *please* don't be retarded when you are closing out your tab. Do me a favor, and say "Hey, I need to close out Rebecca Johnson." It is then, a simple deed for me to walk to my computer, pull up Rebecca Johnson, and charge it to your credit card. When you walk up, after I have already had fifteen *other* idiots do the same thing, and say "Hey, I need to close my tab." **All** you are doing is making the next question that comes out of my mouth drip with sarcasm. *"What's your tab...?"*

So annoying. Like, did you know that you are not the only chick in here? Did you notice that you aren't the only dude in a backwards cap? No? cool. Now I know that the *next* time you are here, your tab will be under *"moron"*.

When going to a bar, it is an absolute necessity that once *at* the bar; you know what it is that you want. Nothing is more infuriating to the busy bartender than some jerk off standing there with a feebleminded expression on their face, asking one of the most insufferable questions of all time. "Um...what do you have...?" My simple reply to this asinine question? "Let me check..." as I walk away and put my fist through a wall.

I cannot remember a time that I walked into a bar not already tasting the cold Miller Lite that I was about to order, followed shortly thereafter by a delectable shot of chilled vodka. It's like **not** knowing what your favorite color is, or looking at the chef and saying "Just make me somethin..." GAAAAA! I would rather put a cigarette out in my eye, than be the chick that wasted forty-five valuable seconds of drinking time by asking such a stupid question. It's a bar honey, what do you *think* we have? Of course, there is another question you can ask that will guarantee you a spot at the bottom of our priority list. It begins with the following seven words; "Do you know how to make a..." *Sigh* Let me guess, you are twenty-one, you have been bartending for six months, and you think that no one else on the planet knows how to make the simple minded concoction that you are currently craving. Let me assure you darling, if it has a name I can make it, and if I can't make it, I can fake it, and you will never know the difference. So please, don't waste my time by asking me if I know how to make your stupid drink, just fucking tell me what you want.

The fourth and final requirement when going to a bar is probably your make or break axiom. KNOW YOUR ROLE. If you are the loud guy, know that every one refers to you as the loud guy. If you are the bar slut, don't get mad when people call you the bar slut! Cougars, stinkies, pool sharks, lushes, barbies, frat boys, meatheads, queens, fat chicks… this applies to all of you. Don't go disturbing the peace and screwing up *our* good time by getting all sensitive on us. You had the opportunity to present a different side of yourself to the pack; unfortunately your actions have landed you under your current title. As inappropriate as it might seem when your boyfriend is there to call you the "bar slut"…don't forget, you have crept on all of the male bartenders, gone home with countless first timers, slept with all of the door guys, *and* you were making out with that random dude in the corner last Tuesday…

Of course, occasionally alcohol wrecks the fun being had at your expense and those of you with the less appealing labels' try to revolt, which only causes you to say or do something that you are going to regret tomorrow. Especially when you wake up to twelve new voicemails, inadvertently finding out that you are now barred for thirty days for punching a good bar friend in the face, telling the owner to go fuck himself, and peeing on the wall in the bathroom. All in all, it is simply in good fun when you earn a title at the bar, or when you are there enough to get one. It's like a twisted *Cheers*… though hopefully without Ted Danson…

Chapter Two
LIKE...OMG...

The Rookies

Ahh, the young and uneducated. To be tender footed and stupid, thinking that we have all the answers only to grow up and find out that we don't even know the questions yet. **Rookie.** Unfortunately for the tenurial, this acronym also pertains to the staff. When you have been toughened by the trials and tribulations of this vexing gig, tact and forbearance aren't always readily available when you find yourself smack in the middle of a busy night with a Rookie at the bar, on the floor, or even worse, *behind* the bar. I once had my boss ask me at six o'clock on a Friday night if I 'minded' training a new girl. Now, mind you, I am the easiest of people to work with, as long as you stay out of my way, don't ask me any questions, and leave me the fuck alone. What makes it even *more* fun you ask? When she walked in and I found out that she was twenty-one years old, fresh out of Bartending School, and had never made a drink in her life, much less waited on an actual *human* before. In case you were wondering about my bosses' plight...yeah, he definitely lost a wheel on the highway that night, tumbled over a cliff, and exploded on impact. The police told us that someone had loosened the lug-nuts on his tires....weird.

I have no problem with Rookies trying to break into the field; after all...who am I going to fuck with when I finally hang up my bottle opener? What my problem with the Rookies is; they suck at life. They don't have to work their asses off anymore to get somewhere, they just have to know someone who knows someone that works at a bar and then there they are, infiltrating a title that you have worked extremely hard at making your own. Sometimes, a Rookie falls ass backwards into a management position, and then *everyone* is fucked. I worked at a place once, where the owner was so tired of being there until dawn every day that he grabbed a twenty-two year old *door guy*, and made him the general manager. Basically, when he was in seventh grade, I was already bartending. Ouch. Taking orders from someone that is more than half your age, doesn't know a liquor cost from a TPS report, and uses Ebonics to write a menu is enough to make you go postal. Literally. Welcome to our Hell.

The Rookies both behind the bar and *at* the bar are easy to spot. They are either ordering strawberry daiquiris or asking how to make them. Either way… it is exasperating. Furthermore, it is the first sign of being an amateur. I'm the kind of girl that avoids the fruit at the brunch buffet, so I certainly don't want it in my tasty beverages. Plus, if you are the one ordering such a thing, have your ID ready, because I am thinking you are on Spring Break…from High School.

The Rookies can be somewhat fun, I suppose, *if* you can find one that's not too annoying. The majority of them, however, are trying *way* too hard to acclimate themselves to their new environment. Starting up conversation when none is necessary, droning on about music or Myspace, reaching out to connect with someone, *anyone* that might make this realm of fast talking veterans a little easier to bear. It's hard to feel bad for them, even though I was once one myself. Unlike most of the newbies, I worked my ass for three years as a waitress. One day, the bartender broke his foot, my manager threw me behind the bar, placing every bit of trust that one can summon, in *me*. I was twenty. I was terrified. For the next week I covered all of the day shifts behind the bar and by the time the broken footed bartender returned, his spot was no longer there for him. I had an undeniable talent for slingin' the booze. It's ok, he was kinda old, and I had nicer boobs. That was twelve years ago. So you can imagine my frustration when some slacker strolls in off the street and writes 'bartender' under the *position applying for* section of an application, followed by 'none' under the *experience* portion of the paper.

The absolute best thing about the Rookies is that they don't fully appreciate the magnitude of the situation. They continuously underestimate the game, and on top of it, they forget they are the pawns. On our down time, we play with them, and it is a hilarious distraction in our somewhat infuriating evening. Sending them off on errands, setting them up for failure, and confusing the ever loving shit out of them. Yes, sadly, it is what we live for. It's almost like we are the Seniors sending the Freshman out on an arduous journey to find the pool on the third floor of the high school… when there *is* no third floor. Basically we are reliving our youth, only this time we are supplied with experience and alcohol. Only one declaration makes this childish conduct acceptable; the ones that are now retired did the same things to us. Besides, it's fucking *fun*.

Sometimes we forget what it is like to be the low man on the totem pole, but rest easy, we will remember that God forbidden emotion the second we set foot behind a new bar. No matter how much experience lies under your belt, there is always *one* person there, ready and willing to remind you just how long they have been pulling the taps at this particular picnic. Trying not to roll your eyes and struggling to smile casually, with the twenty year old waitress barking orders at you, and a Rookie training you on a computer system that you have worked on for six years; it is easy to find your humility. Unfortunately for the waitress, she doesn't know you yet, nor does she understand what a car coated in melted butter and covered with bev-naps will do to a paint job…

In short, as obnoxious as they are, the Rookies play an important part in the ever growing industry that we find ourselves devoted to. Whether they are burdening us with their atrocious queries or forcing us to say "sorry the blender is broken", it would be a sad day for all of us if nobody new ever showed up on the scene. We cannot live without them. I mean, we *could*, but it would only mean one less thing to complain about, and seriously, what fun would that be?

Chapter Three
90210

The Lost Bar Episodes

My oh my, where do I begin? If you have ever set foot in a bar, you have witnessed some drama. The definition of drama is as follows; any situation or series of events having vivid, emotional, conflicting or striking interests or results. Wait… when have you ever seen *that* at the bar? In all honesty, I have been barred from *several* bars, my friends have been barred from *other* bars, my sister has been tossed *out* of bars, and my boyfriend…well, *he* just makes fun of us because he doesn't drink. Technically, as a bartender, I **should** know better than to cause a scene or get out of hand, and for the record, the only time that I have ever made an actual *scene* was in Vegas…and we all know the rules about Vegas.

The drama *at* the bar is nowhere near as exciting as the drama on the other side of it. The cooks are banging the waitresses, the owner is creeping around on his wife with the customers, there are late night conversations over illegal after hours shots, and let's not forget the occasional make out sessions in the walk in between bartenders. The list goes on and on. Not to paint a negative picture, but the restaurant industry is more corrupt than the secret meetings being held in the Oval Office. Just when you think you are safe, ugly exboyfriend shows up and throws a fucking monkey wrench in your well greased cog…

Or... the customer that you went to dinner with "as friends" is now leaving flowers on your car, and the door guy that you accidentally slept with got your name tattooed on his chest.

The fact that no matter *who* is doing *what*, **someone** knows about it, well that just keeps the vicious wheel spinning round and round, and gossip is the gas that powers it. It is a soap opera, and we are the stars. Rest assured that while you are bellied up to the bar, whether the air is as thick as syrup with tension, or everyone is all peaches and cream, **someone** is busting at the seams with jealousy, envy, rage, or vodka... and the fireworks will begin at five after two, as soon as the last customer is safely out the door. I am guilty of this myself, of course. Once, the manager (if you could call him that) of a bar that I was working at, insulted a friend of mine, after I tried to save her from a *creeper* (see following chapter for definition) and he (the manager) who was downright famous for sitting on his fat ass and playing Keno, took sides with the creeper, even after this sicko tried to follow my friend out to her car. I was steaming, but I managed to keep it together until the lights flickered (the oh-so-glorious tell tale sign of last call) and the *second* that door was locked, I started kicking over trash cans and telling my "manager" exactly what he could go do to himself. Yes, it was dramatic, and yes, there was liquor involved, but speaking as my own attorney, I did have a legitimate point... you don't shit on your regulars. *Especially* if they are best friends with the bartender. Curiously enough, I was "transferred" a few weeks later to one of our partner bars, and I ended up quitting because of it. The moral of the story? There isn't one. Just another day at the office. These are the things to be expected of the people that earn their living by flirting shamelessly, smiling through venomous glares, and charming people sneakily out of their cash, while mainlining Smirnoff Orange.

My favorite bar drama is the strange ability that some people possess for making a complete ass out of themselves, while somehow remaining unable of grasping the fact that they, in fact, look like an idiot. I once had a guy sit at the bar for the duration of a Friday night. He ordered shots for every single girl that walked by, grabbed the mic from the deejay, talked incessantly about how much cash he had in his pocket, and told people that he owned the joint, in hopes of striking up conversation and possibly scoring some female companionship for the ride home. And yet, you wouldn't believe the scene that this douche bag made when it came time to pony up the dough. Ranting and raving that we were trying to get one over on him, screaming that we had been sandbagging his tab, oh my Lord it was ridiculous. I was waiting for him to thank the Academy when he was finished. The other bartender and I just laughed and I said "…But you *own* the joint…" In the long run he got exactly what he wanted. Everyone in the room was staring at him. Bravo. Bravo. The standing ovation as he got manhandled by the bouncer made it all worthwhile in the end, for us. Well, that, *and* the eighteen percent gratuity that we added to his tab…

Strangely, bar drama is not too far off from daytime serials or cheesy reality television. There are certain characters that you adore, others that you absolutely despise, a few for comic relief, and finally, the supporting roles. The ones who are there to fill in the background, while providing no real plot twists or surprises. (In bar drama, these are the regulars.) They create no turmoil, no commotion, they are just always there, settled into the bedrock. Appreciated as they are, they are not included in the drama portion of the show. They can be counted upon for excellent recaps of any given evening, great tips, good laughs, and very few spectacles. Thankfully, they too live by the most essential rule of our existence; don't shit where you eat.

When you work in an environment that requires you to interact with many different kinds of people on a daily basis, it is difficult not to develop certain relationships. Some of these relationships can be casual "Hey, how is the wife"… while others are a tad more pronounced. The waitress that you tell exaggerated life stories to, the bar back that you hate, the creepy door guy who always hints around to an obscure sexual encounter, and last but not least, the one you shouldn't have a crush on but find yourself thinking about anyway. *This* always creates the drama. Whether you are acting on it or pretending that you don't even notice them, it is stewing just beneath the surface, just waiting for the opportunity to blow up and embarrass you, or get you into trouble. *Hating* certain people has the same outcome. No matter *what* this person is doing, it is aggravating the hell out of you. Even if you swore that you would never get involved in the politics, you find yourself spouting off a list of things that they have done to irritate you, to anyone that will listen. Then *that* person tells someone else, while bullshitting on a smoke break, and thus… the exciting series of counterfeit accounts begins. By the time this chain of rumors has run its course, I will have murdered this botherment by grinding up glass, slipping it into their drink, and watching happily as the shards slowly cut their intestines until they *died*.

When bar drama takes over the enterprise, *especially* when the innuendo centers around management or the owners, you will begin to notice the schedule changing ever so slightly. People that worked five shifts are now down to two, those who used to work every weekend night are now only scheduled for Sunday mornings. This is the strategic way that the powers that be filter out the commentators, once again restoring peace to the galaxy. It's like Noah, and that whole flood thing. Frantically, you scan your brain for any inclination of involvement in these silly escapades. Trying desperately to recall that *one* night that you drank just a tad too much and ended up in a forgotten conversation with the GM about the other managers and their 'extra-curricular' activities. That's when you find yourself clinging to a door like Jack-what's-his-name from Titanic, and praying that the snobby debutant isn't there to kick you off of it, sending you to your icy grave. It is unavoidable, it is archaic, sometimes malicious, mostly hearsay, but always there, bobbing along, just waiting to be discussed…by everyone.

Chapter Four
EEEEK!!!

Stalkers of the world UNITE....

This chapter is solely dedicated to the *creepers*. I'm not sure where or when my girlfriends and I were when we came up with the term 'creeper', but as you can imagine, we were being harassed by one or more men with the distinct ability to give you the all over goose bumps...and *not* the good kind. I am not being egotistical when I say that I have actually had a man sitting at the bar crying, literally *begging* me to go out with him. Incredibly, he seemed unaware of the fact that he was surrounded by people pointing, laughing, and ridiculing him. This guy worked for a *universally* known aeronautical administration, was divorced, and had two kids. He came into my bar every single afternoon for about three years. I had no idea that he harbored such intense affections towards me until one day, I was leaving Starbucks, with two delicious lattes' in hand, and I heard someone call my name. As I looked around, I saw no one that I knew or even recognized. Shrugging off this strange incident, I proceeded to my Blazer, toting the two coffees' that I had just purchased, for myself and my hetero-lifemate, who was at that moment, babysitting my very young son. As I neared my truck, I noticed that there was someone leaning against it. I was slightly confused, and at first I didn't even recognize him. And that's when he hit me with it. The unexpected declaration of love. For months he persisted, following me to concerts, buying me gifts, taking my picture from across the room, writing me poetry and publishing it in our local newspaper. At first, I will admit, it was kind of flattering. Give me a break, I was only twenty. I had never before been exposed to the sort of lifestyle that revolved around people putting me up on pedestals, hanging on every word I said, and thinking that I was the most amazing person that ever lived. And then I became acutely aware of the fact that I was never alone. He literally knew where I lived, every place that I hung out, knew what my boyfriend drove, and all the places that I shopped. It became such a problem, that I eventually quit that job and then went on to work at the most awesome bar on the planet. He tried to follow me to that bar also, but thankfully, my manager barred him for life after a particularly psychotic outburst where he began pulling out his hair and screaming *"why don't you love me!?"* at the top of his lungs, breaking shot glasses on the bar and waving his limbs around like a retarded member of the Village People. One of my best friends to this day still tells that story. (After all, It was *his* shot glass that the stalker grabbed, and smashed on the bar...) Mayhem. I'm sure in his own deranged mind he had created a relationship between us, even though it was completely one sided. Over the years, I have become more accustomed to such bizarre demeanor, as it happens more often than you would think. When you are a female, no matter what size, shape or color, you are spending your afternoons fighting off unwanted advances. In the grocery store at nine in the morning, clad in sweatpants and glasses, you still notice guys tailing you from aisle to aisle, offering to help with the top shelf items that you can't quite reach. It is clever, but to the guarded woman, these efforts are thwarted by an instinctive defense mechanism. It's called a fart. The message is simple; Get away from me *you fucking creeper*! I'm not sure exactly what makes them do it. Maybe it is the long lost caveman lurking inside of them, but for whatever reason, the penis bearing members of society just can*not* control their carnal impulses.

The *sneaky creepers* are of a different sort. *These* Guys try to befriend unsuspecting lambs with bogus sentiment and false bravado. Pretending not to be interested, as they stealthily lay the ground work for invasion… common interests, mutual friends, the blasé laid back manner in which they calculate their attack. It is combative. It is plotted and indefensible. I unknowingly succumbed to the trickery of such a sly fox, in my more recent years, and much to my surprise, found myself swept up into an emotional tornado of epic proportions. Fueled by booze, punctuated by sex, involuntarily allowing myself to be tossed into a whirlwind affair. Betting on pool games, shooting knowing glances across the bar, texting even though we were in the same room, slipping notes to each other, sneaking out the back door of the bar for a quick make out… doing pirouettes on a razor thin line between reality and ecstasy. Naturally, it ended abruptly when I discovered that he had been creeping on a slightly younger, dumber model, that he actually had the audacity to bring into my bar, *while* we were still 'dating'. It happens. Only the **Supremely** protected woman holds the Kryptonite for *that* kind of villain.

The word 'creep' is the foundation for the expression *creeper*; to move slowly with the body close to the ground, as a reptile or insect, or a person on hands and knees. Definitions can be so scary. Especially when they are being proven fifteen times a night, by the degenerate skulking in the corner, that has already memorized your name, bra size, and license plate number, and who will most likely be hiding in your bushes when you get home tonight…

As the object of adoration, we reserve the right to refuse intimacy; yet, this gesture does not always seem to compute. When dealing with a *persistent creeper* we must remember to approach with caution. Smiling and talking calmly, as not to anger the beast. It's almost like we are on Safari… Not only is this frustrating, it is time consuming. Naturally, over the course of our evenings, it becomes necessary to stroke the egos of the men who continuously empty their pockets, but more often than not, this proves to be the most difficult of tasks. **Yes**, we want you to stay. **Yes**, we want you to have a good time. **Yes**, we want you to tip double and sign over the deed to your boat. *But*, we do **not** want you to wait for us in the parking lot and offer us a ride home. We do **not** want to come to your cookout. And we sure as Hell do **not** want to go to the mall and pick out new shirts with you. Sometimes just having a drink and relaxing before going home to that wife that you complain about, is enough…for both of us. *Sigh* some people just don't understand the separation between business and pleasure. **We do.**

Don't think for a second that I am going to leave the *female* creepers out of this twisted little equation. For any male bartender, bar back, cook, manager, bouncer or owner, you poor bastards suffer one of the most agonizing creeper categories *ever*. The *Desperate Creeper*. These are the women that go the bar *alone*. They might start out as fun loving, outgoing dancing queens- but as the night wears on and the shots continue to flow, they gradually cross over into prowler mode. Ever seen *Silver Bullet*? Yeah, well, the transformation isn't quite that graphic, but it's equally scary. The closer to last call it gets, the more eager they become, and the hungrier they are to sink their teeth into the kill…

By the way, if you are the kill it means that you have abandoned all efforts being made by your friends, ignored every warning from the bartenders, walked past the snickering door guys, and have by your own elixir induced decision making process come to the conclusion that getting into a car with this she-devil will somehow result in a happy ending. Yes, you might have a wild bout of kinky sex, and perhaps it *will* end up in a mutual understanding that the 'one night stand' rules actually apply, *but*, I can pretty much guarantee that you now have a chick that is cyber stalking you and driving past your house three times a week. I know, I know. It makes a bad name for the rest of the women in the bar, and I hate to say I told you so, but…

Let's not forget the *Geezer Creepers*. These guys are just plain old perverts. *"Oh, if I was twenty years younger, you would be in trouble…"* No…if you were twenty years younger I could punch you in the face without feeling guilty about it. While most of these poor, washed up drunks are harmless, there are some of them that choose to cross the line, *frequently*. I can't tell you how many times I have been caught up in a conversation about my boobs, without knowing that the discussion had changed so unexpectedly from the previous one. Believe me it is not as blatant as "*Hey, did you see that bullshit inauguration speech that the President gave yesterday...*" "*You've got great tits*"... Whoa. No, instead they sneak it in on you like a ninja planting a bomb in your brain stem, and you don't really even know that they have said anything inappropriate until you have set their refilled draft on the coaster in front of them, and walked away. *That's* when you are at the computer, pulling up a tab, and then suddenly, in the back of your mind you are like *wait a second...did he just...* Yes, yes he did. And on top of it, he gets away with it. Why? Because he is older than dirt, and if you waste your time getting pissed about it, it doesn't matter anyway, because the end result is the same. He will walk out on his tab (when you *think* he has only gone to the bathroom, for the eighty second time of the night) *and* he will be back tomorrow. For some insane reason, these guys never get kicked out. Don't get me wrong, they have been asked to *leave*, but they never get booted out. They usually know the owner, or are friends with Jesus, because everyone seems to turn their heads when this old ass canker gets one too many beers in him, and starts acting a fool.

Come on down! Our next disgusting contestant on the *Get the Fuck Away From Me* show is... *The Management Creeper*... Whether he is the owner, GM, kitchen manager, or head of security, *this* guy is checking out every chick on the payroll. Screening applications, reveling in the interview process, lining up perspective 'hookups', the Master of the House can always be counted upon to fill up a few key positions, and then simply stock the hen house with easy pickings' for the rest of the wolves... The management creeper is a little harder to derail, since you have to pick and choose your battles. When there are plenty of witnesses, you make act sheepish or naïve, but when you are the last one to leave, and your spider sense is reverberating with the *creeper* vibe, it is absolutely necessary to stand your ground... if not, you will be the chick that is sleeping with the higher power, and before you know it, *everyone* will be chatting about it. Remember the chapter before this one? Yeah...that will be you...

To any female working in this nauseating industry, the *Beware of the Creeper* documentary *should* be shown to you on your very first day. However, this knowledge must be EARNED. After a few years of waiting tables and putting up with the scum of skid row, you might finally be equipped with the basic weaponry required to ward off the predators long enough to stumble behind the bar for the first time. But, only packing the heat of experience (which means shuffling through nine hundred customers a night, weeding out the somewhat undesirable conversationalists) do you totally possess the ability to foil the superfluous intentions of the notorious creeper. After many, many years of not knowing *quite* how to handle certain ogling and relentless lurkers, you finally have acquired the skills and the *balls* to just say *"Hey...Fuck you..."*

Chapter Five
DATING A BARTENDER

"...Dude, that's my girlfriend...."

Anyone that works in this ungodly business knows one, if not two things for certain… One, being that chivalry is, in fact, *dead*. (Even if it is not clear in our own relationships, we witness it, in all its glory-in every way definable. Men sneaking to the bar after work to shop for casual sex. Guys leaving their women *at* the bar, guys bringing different women *to* the bar, *and* guys mistreating the chicks that are already there. I mean, in no way are we innocent as a gender, but, I have never heard anyone utter the phrase; *Women* are pigs…) And Two, it is pretty much common knowledge that an alternate set of rules apply for dating *bartenders*, as we are of a different feather altogether…

Incredulously, our species actually finds a way to interact and mate with a certain selected few from the other side. I know, I know, *what* the hell are we thinking, right..? Someone who doesn't drink, hang out at bars, or spend their evenings joshing over pool games and starting fights over spilled pitchers...? *Where* in the world do we find such gems..? I will elaborate. They are either the men that we already love coming into this game… we somehow luck out while shopping in the organic section at the local market… *or* we manage to stumble upon Mr. Right while cruising the bookstore for the latest Koontz hardback. *I* lucked out by finding a gloriously hot guy, who not only *doesn't* drink, but literally despises being around drunken idiots *so* much, that he just flat out refuses to go near the bar. Therefore, I never have to worry about him boozing it up at my bar, on *my* dollar, making a scene, throwing up, or getting jealous of the endless wave of retards washing up on the sands of delirium.

I must give credit where credit is due, and hand out fictional awards to those brave and broadminded souls that have somehow evaded murder charges, even though they are in a relationship with an individual that earns their cash in this all consuming business. It is complete havoc, even more so to the guy or girl who leads a quasi-normal life. When you come home in a bad mood, *literally* walk in the door bitching, about the complete and total lack of order, your face twisted in disdain, seething and rummaging through cupboards and refrigerator drawers, griping loudly, while searching aimlessly for even a *drop* of booze...This amazing person manages to talk you back to reality. I swear I have put my boyfriend through the wringer twice a week for the past five years.

When dating a bartender, there are a few things that you have to remember. The first being, that we are *surrounded* by men. Drunken men, horny men, stupid men, stalker men...But, just because we are swimming in a sea of cylindrical organs does *not* mean that we are tempted to grab onto a passing fish and go for a ride. Just because someone *wants* to sleep with us, doesn't mean that they actually *get* to. Flirting comes with the territory, and should be considered nontoxic to the relationship. It's like a piece of flair, a uniform requirement that we don't like to wear or talk about. So ignore it, because it means nothing more than a few extra twenties in the tip bucket at the end of the night...

If you are actually stupid enough to hang out at your significant others' bar, you can expect to be irritated the *entire* time. Even if you are a descendant of that rare breed of non-jealous males, you will undoubtedly encounter that *one* person that just rubs you the wrong way. Suddenly, your girl is in between you and this guy, the bouncer has his arm around your neck, and you are being dragged towards the front door, while shouting "Come outside dude! Come outside!" It is unfortunate, and unavoidable. And it ends up right in the bar drama rolodex under boyfriend do's and don'ts. What *should* you do? Stay home.

Another thing to keep in mind is that we **drink**. You almost never find anyone in this business that is on the wagon. Trust me, even the underage cooks have a pitcher of beer hidden behind the line *somewhere*. But **because** we are in the public service industry, it is basically a *requirement*. Otherwise, we would be committed to the local asylum, mummified with saran wrap or incarcerated in one of those awfully taboo jackets with all of the buckles, threatening to scratch out our eyes…or yours…

When I say we drink, I mean we *drink*. We drink while we are working, we drink at home. We seek out places that are serving booze at 6 am, and we usually have a bottle of something chilling in the freezer. So, if you are a recovering alcoholic, dating a bartender is out of the question. *For both of us.* Trust me, the last thing we need when we get home at three in the morning is finding the 12 Step Program sponsors collected in the living room, sitting in the classic intervention circle, waiting to tell us how our lives are being controlled by evil alcohol. Seriously, we don't say "Hey, what's your poison..?" because we are *unaware* that liquor is bad for you, we just don't *care*. In fact, I rather enjoy my kidneys hurting and my decision making abilities being revoked by the devil at the bottom of the vodka bottle… It keeps it interesting.

There are a few annoying qualities that we possess also, and even though we are conscious of them, we continue to do them anyway. For example, when watching a movie with a bartender, any bottle of alcohol glimpsed in the film is immediately identified, *out loud*. Don't ask me, I don't know why. It's like we are compelled by some alien force to impress the 'others' with our knowledge of the booze. Ever find yourself caught up in a conversation about whiskey or wine when you don't really care about the alcohol content or where it's imported from? Sorry. It's a nasty little habit. Just like when we are at a bar, some of the more annoying members of our little dysfunctional society find it necessary to inform the bartender, that they are *also* a bartender. (That one I am *not* guilty of, because, well, it irritates the crap out of me.) Yeah, we know a lot about alcohol. Is it annoying? Yep. But I'm sure you talk about *your* job at great length, and minus the exciting details, so, shut up...

Also, we have a different concept of *time*. We go by how many shots we have had, not by the clock on the wall. If your bartender has worked the day shift, and says she will be home in an hour... just go to bed, because she will not stumble through the door until midnight, at least. It's not our fault. Honestly. We have *every* intention of coming home as soon as we get off, unfortunately, we are easily persuaded to sit down, relax, and have a beer. One beer. This turns into two beers, and a shot. Before we know it, we are pumping dollars into the jukebox, caught up in a girl's verses guy's pool tournament, quoting 'The Hangover' and telling racist jokes... To make it worse, (or *better*, depending on which view point you are looking at it from) someone keeps buying *more* shots... And, let's face it, *no one* wants to be the party pooper when the boss is the one buying round after round, in a wicked attempt to avoid going home, even though his wife has called the bar numerous times *and* threatened some sort of violence...

When dating a bartender you also have to understand the sleep schedule. Get ready to be employed as my alarm clock, because I will be the first to tell you that I am *not* getting out of bed before two. So if you are calling, and my voicemail picks up sixty-seven times in a row- first of all, you are border lining on creeper crazy- and secondly, you just don't know the night that I have had. The only thing more important than my sleep is the way that I do it. Like all of us night crawlers, my bed is my haven. Decked out in feather pillows, down comforters and four million thread count sheets. Butter. So you can imagine how difficult it might be to climb out of something so comfortable, unless there is a really, *really* good reason. (Meeting your mom at eight o'clock on a Saturday morning does not qualify as a good reason. Hell, I won't even get out of bed to meet my *own* mother that early, so if you want us to meet, sweetie, pick a decent hour…) Also, you can*not* ask your bartender to brunch, if brunch ends at three. Brunch needs to be an all day event, with eggs and bacon out until at least six o'clock, with mimosa's and Bloody Mary's flowing until you guys are ready for bed and she is ready for work. It is just the way it is. Welcome to the life.

Another thing about dating one of these unruly beverage serving foxes, is, that if you *ever* challenge her on the importance of her profession, she will turn on you like a viper. Don't you *dare* tell her that her life behind the bar is a joke, or a walk in the park. Just because you spend your afternoons aerating some old lady's lawn, programming a computer, or mining for coal- doesn't mean that you could ever be man enough to stand behind that bar and pour a drink… much less fourteen hundred of them…so sit back, shut up, and be appreciative of your drink mixing vixen…it is hard enough to catch one and call her your own, but even harder still, to **keep** her.

Chapter Six
THE REVOLVING DOOR

"Whose Table is it anyway....?"

The Staff. Ugh. You probably have interoffice relationships that have lasted for years. I, on the other hand, refuse to even learn the new girls name unless she stays for a month. The turnover rate for employees in bars and restaurants is the equivalent of how often normal people change their underwear. The cocktail waitress that started on Tuesday will have quit by Friday. The bouncer that started last month has been let go for the fight that his girl started in the bar on his night off last Wednesday. The new bartender caught wind that the old bartenders didn't like her and she didn't show up for work on Saturday night. The Monday night deejay got into a fight with a regular on football Sunday, and has been replaced with the Thursday night shooter girl, who has been dying to get into the booth for six months. Meanwhile, every single day, eight different people show up and ask if we are hiring, filling out applications in hopes of being given a chance to be the next one to take the title...*newbie*. I'm not kidding, this actually happens.

The tight knit cliques that form in the bar, spill out into real life as well. Some of my best girlfriends to this day, are chicks that have taken the field of battle with me. When you spend that much time together, especially when there is alcohol involved, you are bound to bond with a few people. Guys are included in this situation also, and not just the gay one's. Enemies form in this scenario too. Not just co-workers, but regulars, and friends of co-workers as well. I have definitely come to *highly* despise a select few semi-humans during my experiences behind the bar.

There are also people that you just don't *get*. I work with a kid that is training to be a cage fighter, or a ring fighter or whatever they are called. He is super strange, really awkward, and pretty dumb. He must get hit in the head a lot, because everything that comes out of his mouth is in one way or another *confusing*. I have to spend fifteen minutes sifting through the jumbled mess of words, just to decipher the *real* reason he opened up his stupid trap in the first place. It's annoying as hell, so now I just insult him, in hopes that he won't even talk to me, therefore I don't have to employ my brain as much, while trying to shake up shots and remember the thirty-two drinks that I have to make in five minutes flat. Same goes for the ultra bubbly, touchy feely waitress that decided we were best friends a few seconds into her second training shift. Fortunately, I was off the night that she started, because from what I hear she didn't shut up about herself the entire time. Gag. I have never really tried to make friends at work, which, I suppose, is why it happens so quickly. I mean, it's unusual to see someone that tries as desperately to get attention from *anyone*, as this chick. Good lord, she hugs everyone that walks into the room, asks a million and one questions about your personal life, and talks your fucking ear off, even when you are flat out *ignoring* her. Jesus Christ, she is like a doped-up-ankle-biting Pekingese, humping my leg and begging for table scraps. But, thankfully, she got really hungry, because she moved away to go to culinary school. Whew, side stepped a land mine…don't think I could have controlled the devil in me for too much longer. I have a trillion stories about people that I have encountered over the years, and believe me there isn't enough time to tell them all.

I have been employed at every position up the ladder, from hostess to manager, and I can tell you, that the latter is probably the worst. Having to babysit twenty different people per shift is enough to make you want to hunker down in the office, put on some Mozart, and guzzle a deadly cocktail of Clorox and Jack Daniels. Hiring, firing, training, counseling, coaching...It's *draining*.

The staff is composed of a highly complex -diverse if not disorderly- band of rebels that are, without question, slaves to the grind. The papoose's are the ones who are just starting out, or just passing through, trying to determine what exactly they want to *be* when they 'grow up'. While they are here, they learn inside lingo, develop the insatiable greed for the almighty dollar that this lifestyle revolves around, and hopefully pick up a few people skills along the way. The Drifters are the ones who come in and out of the biz, one day they are washing dishes and then the next, they are doing construction for their old man's company. They casually float in and out, taking odd jobs just like any normal nomad. These are the awesomely cool guys that, when they land themselves in the right place, shock everyone with their broad talents of bar backing and cooking, whilst washing dishes, painting walls, and re-hanging wooden trim (they are usually stoners though, so watch your stash or cash, because they will pocket that shit and you won't see them again until you decide to go bowling one day, and lo and behold, they will be the guy cooking your fries at the snack bar.) We, on the other hand, are the *lifers*. The ones who have been doing it forever, and will continue on in the biz, until we make our inevitable approach toward decrepitude. Whatever takes us out, will no doubt be affiliated with this world that we have come to know, live, and love... The Bar Life. Whether it is a heart attack from an over dose of No-Doz or downing twelve Red Bull's in attempt to stay awake for the last hour of a treacherous Friday night, an obscure and unprecedented incident involving alcohol poisoning, falling off of a roof, murdered by a passionate stalker, **or,** the dreaded slayer of alkies; Cirrhosis. We will not go out, *unless* we go out in a blaze of glory... Surrounded solemnly by partners' in crime, who are holding up Bic lighters, pounding shots of their fallen friends' liquor of choice, telling stories of their beloved sidekicks' unruly antics, and laughing through the tears. Clinking glasses, merrily rejoicing in what they used to know of the good times, with Freddie Mercury serenading them from beyond the grave, with the lyrics from "Another one bites the dust…"

Either way, it is safe to say that you have never encountered such a contrasting collection of charisma and character, in any of the other walks of life. I mean simply, that you probably aren't going to find a group of joke telling, beer slinging bandits behind the popcorn counter at the movie theatre…

Chapter Seven
STRANGE BREW

The Adult Teddy Bear

Beer. Mmmmm, the delicious and refreshing. Ales, Lagers, Draughts, Stouts, Bocks, Pilsners, Micro Brews, Pale Ales, Porters, Belgian Wheat's, IPA's, Ice's, Golden's, Dark's, Lite's..So many options, so little time. I love a man who loves his beer. I love a *woman* who loves her beer, more. Beer is the icebreaker in many situations. When the new guy at the office is trying to bond with co-workers, he doesn't ask them to go horseback riding, does he? No. He says "Hey…anyone want to grab a bottle of suds..?" When being invited to a party, you don't ask if there will be a tray of carrots… You ask whether it's BYOB, or not. When you are sitting at the bar by yourself, and some random stranger sits down next to you, orders the same beer that you are currently enjoying yourself, a strange little nod of appreciation passes between the two of you, thus enticing a conversation that could last twenty seconds or two hours, and **bam**, you have either made a new friend or met your soul mate. I've seen it a hundred times. So, what is this instigator of camaraderie all about?

Well, it's simple. Different grains, herbs, oats, hops, spices, and starches are fermented together at various temperatures, following an assortment of recipes. And the end result is the glorious inebriant that comes in a wonderful array of sizes and colors. Some people prefer draft. Some like their bottles. Some like beer so thick you can't see through the glass. Some enjoy it warm. Some would rather it be served icy cold. It is amazing the choices that are offered for the consumption of this simply made and simply savored brew. There are countless books, movies, poems, songs, and even stores, dedicated *entirely* to beer. I can only think of a few other things in the world that are as widely appreciated as beer, but none of them are as G rated.

Draft beer is generally a Happy Hour special in every bar around the globe. With draft beer the possibilities for **specials** are endless. Because the cheaper keg's cost about twelve bucks, you can get away with serving quarter pints, penny pitchers, even beer by the inch. The latter is my favorite, because it challenges people to use their imagination. They bring in their own apparatus, and you charge anywhere from twenty five to seventy five cents per inch of beer. The public responds to this challenge with creativeness and excellent problem solving skills. They bring in the largest, flattest things that they can find in their kitchen, to get the most beer for their coins. Everything is fine and dandy, until the extra *crafty* guy walks in with an inflatable baby pool under his arm, a ruler in his pocket, and demands that you fill it up exactly two inches…

This valuable commodity brings people together in social environments from here to Timbuktu. Some groups of people, old or young, get together *every single* afternoon to share a pint and lighthearted conversation. The always identifiable sound of mugs clinking mugs, loud music, playful banter, and laughter, go hand in hand with gaiety. Even to people that *don't* drink, this harmonious cacophony cannot be construed as anything other than absolute delight. I don't have a thousand words about beer, but, because I love it so much, I thought it would be nice to toss a half a page of praise to our always dependable friend. I often write this phrase when I am having a bad day, and on more than one occasion, it has been my Facebook status for days at a time; **Remember, no matter how bad things get in life, there is always beer…**

Chapter Eight
THE SEND BACKS

"…This tastes like juice…"

Three simple words for anyone that sends back a drink. I hate you. You are the reason that bartenders are so evil. Let me assure you, if you ordered a Sex on the Beach, then that is *exactly* what I made for you. If you wonder why it tastes like that, well, it's because you ordered a Sex on the fucking BEACH! It is raspberry, melon, and pineapple juice. Yeah, that shit is reserved for teenagers. Why not order a shot? Or a beer? Instead of a drink that has a combined alcohol content of two percent… Wonder why you don't have a buzz? Hmmmmm….

Seriously, we are not responsible for your bad taste, so why on earth do you give us those smug little smiles, when standing before us, questioning our ability to do our job? I absolutely *loathe* you. Let me give you an example of lunkhead behavior.

Idiot (you); "Hi, can I have a vodka and cranberry?"
Bartender; "Four dollars."
The exchange is made, the sip is taken.
Idiot (you); "Um, this tastes' like *juice.*"

And that's it. Right there. That's all it takes for us. That tiny little predicament, and suddenly we are wishing for a cartoon piano to fall out of the sky and pulverize you. Unfortunately, we are not encouraged to leap across the bar and wrap ourselves around you like a monkey, biting at your jugular and screaming at the top of our lungs **"that's because there is fucking *juice* in it!!!!"** On top of it, for God only knows *what* reason, you retards actually have the audacity to get angry at *us*. How is that possible? *You* ordered it, *you* drank it, the idiotic observation came out of *your* mouth, so in what way are we to blame? Oh, wait a minute, I forgot. You ordered the vodka and *vodka flavored* cranberry juice. Yeah, sorry, we are fresh out of that. Incredibly, this ridiculous behavior repeats itself *all... night... long.*

But wait, there's **more**. When you are doing *service bar*, whether it's at a nightclub, diner, sports bar, or steakhouse, the complaints differ from those of the simpletons sitting *at* the bar. These returns vary depending on the *price* of the drinks that you are sending out. Sometimes, the five ounce pour of expensive Beaujolais is actually only four and a half ounces (don't ask me how these people know this- I suspect that they are carting around a ruler in the breast pocket of their suit jacket.) And sometimes the snifter cradling a portion of Remy Martin doesn't quite seem like enough for the table where Mr. & Mrs. Mc*Greedy* are sitting...

Occasionally, the returns are because of fruit flies, flat soda, bad juice, or bitter beer face. This is the *only* time that it is okay to toss out booze. While these things can be avoided, they are kind of par for the course, and you just have to comp the drink, smile, and then pour another. Hopefully, it was as elementary as one of these reasons, and you aren't dealing with the unsatisfiable buyer. These are the ones who will send back anything and everything, in their never ending quest for freebies. You know the type, they eat the entire meal before "finding" a hair in their mashed potatoes, or slurp down two cosmopolitan's before suddenly deciding that they aren't being made to their liking. I actually enjoy these people. As impossible as they are, they make for great fun, and every owner or manager hates them too. So, if you make one too many carefully observed Long Island Iced Tea's for them, and *snap*, tossing a drink in their face and cussing them out isn't as frowned upon as it would be in a normal situation. *And* when they threaten to never return to the establishment, the owner then gives you a raise for your awful behavior, naming you employee of the month for finally getting rid of the bitch that complains about everything from the paper towels in the ladies room being too rough for her sensitive hands, to the music being too loud, to the air conditioning not being cold enough, therefore frizzing up her expensive hairdo.

The *picky* send backs are the worst. "Well, if Daisy didn't make this, then I don't want it." Uh..ok..? Some people take the job of supporting their regular bartender to the extreme. Others have a different preference of who makes their drinks, and it has nothing to do with regularity. I had a server bring back a gin and tonic *four* times, saying that the woman said "it just doesn't taste right." So, I made another one and told the waitress to tell this impossible woman that a *different* bartender had fixed the drink. It turned out that the woman was watching from across the room, and all at once, the reason for her send backs became obvious. She was instantly *emphatic* about not wanting 'white' bartenders making her drinks. Now, while dancing on this delicate topic, it is crucial to remember that not everyone shares opinions, beliefs, and open-mindedness with the rest of the world, so it has the potential to be a very perilous situation. Of course, I let my temper get the best of me, and when the woman stormed up to the wait station window, slamming her drink down and spilling gin all over my service counter, I began to get a tad sour. I already had four glasses of gin and tonic sitting there, ice melting, that I was going to have to hurriedly sell, or inevitably trash, and somehow explain to my boss *why* exactly I had four Tanqueray's on one spill tab, (because then it looks like I am giving them away) But on top of it, I have a huge angry woman trying to start a fight with me. Swerving her head, and waving her hands at me, she insisted that someone else make her a drink. Unfortunately, I had downed a few cocktails myself, so I swerved and waved back. I proceeded to tell her that the only bartenders that were working were white, and that if she wanted to wait for a different one, she was going to be there for a minute. The argument carried on for a while, where we exchanged a few insults, and "opinion's". Needless to say…she left…*without* paying for the five gins that she ordered, but, she left on the arm of a bouncer that finally noticed the decibel level had gone up two points, then became aware of her absurdity, and escorted her to the door.

Certain things *always* come back. Dirty Bong Water, 1-900-fuk-me-up, Georgia Peach, Apple Jack, Baltimore Zoo, Bonecrushers… these are just a few examples of the complicated drinks we must memorize, and not everyone makes all of them the same way. I will be honest, on some of them, I take the lazy approach. Make it strong and red, and they will like it. It's not that we don't know what goes in it, we just don't fucking feel like picking up twelve bottles to make it. But, more often than not, the reason for the send back is the *name*. Customers obviously frequent a different bar, which means different bartenders. I don't make a Dirty Bong Water the same way as George in the Tavern down the street makes his, or like Julio at the trendy bar in San Diego makes *his*. I mean, it's not like ordering a BLT, when you know that you are getting bacon, lettuce, and tomato with mayo on some form of bread. There are just too many options when it comes to alcohol. That's why *I* stick to the basics. Vodka and beer. Can't mess that up, no matter how hard you try. Occasionally, you get the people that order a drink, and create their own name for it. A Purple Hooter shooter suddenly becomes a Ray Lewis Sack, and a Blue Motor Cycle is now called Baby Blue Cotton Candy. How in the world do we keep up..? We don't. I *used* to say "Hang on, I will see if anyone else has ever heard of it", and actually go ask the other bartenders. That was in my earlier years. Nowadays, I simply make them whatever the hell I want to. It's only fair. Same goes for the blender. It is *always* broken, so don't even bother to order a Pina Colada, or a frozen Margarita, you would probably just send it back any way.

Sometimes I think about going to my eye doctors' office and returning a set of contacts that I have already worn, and smile as I tell him that the reason for my doing so is because "I just don't like them." I want to cause a scene when he tells me that he cannot refund my money, because I have already *worn* them, therefore, they are now **mine**. I also fantasize about setting out for Target, with a used pair of underwear, bought in *their* lingerie department, and then becoming irate because they refuse to exchange them for a new pair, one that might fit a little better, or maybe, I just decided that I no longer like the color of those particular panties. I will ask to speak to a manager, and explain that while I originally thought that I wanted these panties, after wearing them, I have suddenly changed my mind, and I would like something else instead; Maybe a pair of shoes, or a washing machine (which is the equivalent of not liking a shot of Popov and asking for a Belvedere instead.) And then, when the manager looks at me like I have lobsters crawling out of my ears, and asks what exactly is he supposed to do with a pair of used panties, I will say, "Well, idiotic customers come in to *my* place of employment *every day*, and take sips out of drinks that they themselves decided to order, and then they send it back, forcing me to throw away **more** alcohol, and then they complain that they have to pay for another drink...so I just assumed that I could come in here and do it too." I ALSO, would like to go to the liquor store, buy a bottle of vodka and a six pack, walk outside, drop it, and then go back inside and tell them that I need another one... I will just tell their manager to put it on a 'spill check'. I mean, their only reason for existing is to cater to my every whim and desire right? Who cares that what I am saying is ridiculous? These are the illusions that run on a reel to reel in my head, making me laugh, and making it just a tad easier to pretend that I don't want to stab you in the neck with a corkscrew every time you send back a cocktail.

Every once in a while, I feel a little Froggy, and I decide to enforce the rule. What rule you ask? The *Golden* rule of patronage; *don't fuck with the people who handle your food*. Yes, we all saw **Waiting**. Allow me to reaffirm Ryan Reynolds, this rule is very true. Whether you are at Ruth's Chris ordering a steak, or at the dive bar around the corner, just be happy with what you get and be quiet.

Why..? Because you never know what kind of **maniac** is inconspicuously squirting magnesium citrate into your drink, standing back with their arms folded across their chest, a strange little smile on their face, just *waiting* for you to run out of the bar, duck legged, with one arm clutching your stomach, and the other covering the seat of your pants, in attempt to be discreet about the sudden onslaught of bodily functions that you are experiencing.

Basically, the point I am not so subtly trying to relay is; sending back a drink that I have concocted is an insult, a personal attack on my beverage fashioning capability. I feel completely well within my right to react as any artist would; Unleashing quiet lunacy, torturing you with various acts of assassination, stealing your spirit and dispatching you slowly by happily handing over EPICAC cocktails so that you vomit on yourself unexpectedly, or dumping 151 in your drinks *guaranteeing* that you will not be able to perform later, even if you have scored a ride home with the hottest girl in the bar. When the dreaded Whiskey Dick ruins your evening... Just remember that you were the one that first threw down the gauntlet.

Chapter Nine
CURRENT AFFAIRS

Conversation for Dummies...

It has been said that there are two things that you just don't talk about at the bar. Religion and politics. I could honestly name a few more things that you *really* shouldn't discuss, but for now, let's just stick to the basics. In my opinion, religion is only a sore subject for two kinds of people. The super religious and the atheists. I float somewhere in the middle, so chatting it up about how much I hate Eve for placing a rabid cat in my uterus once a month is no biggie. The same goes for questioning the facts, doubting the Faith, and calmly debating the probability of Evolution against Intelligent Design. I can also yap it up about the Presidential candidates, military strategies, or join in those still making fun of the fact that The Terminator is now the Governor of the great state of California. I am unbiased, easy going, and somewhat knowledgeable. The things that interest me have nothing to do with God or the White House, so I am safe. However- having been the one responsible for breaking up a fight between two guys that are too drunk and too old to even throw a punch, is the reason that I write this chapter.

Listen up guys- playful repartee is appreciated, and even the occasional outburst can be overlooked if not condoned, but seriously...C'mon now... Enough of the Left Wing, Right Wing, Ecclesiastes, and Genesis deliberating. It is all just a junior varsity scrimmage to see who can offer up the most improvable evidence, talk the loudest, or piss off the most people with tendentiously preached propaganda.

I am *all for* a heartfelt debate. I also like to embellish in a good old fashioned heated argument. Sometimes, I get just a teeny bit out of hand, and throw out a controversial subject...just to get the blood flowing and the ball rolling in a different direction. Usually this makes me the center of attention, because they are all waiting for some remarkably astounding revelation that I am absolutely *incapable* of making, and, sadly, I end up looking like an idiot. I forget what I was saying, or pull too quick of a switcheroo on the already-fucked-up sponge's, that sit clinging to their warm, hour old beer, confusing them and sending their mind off into yet *another* incomprehensible jumble of thoughts.. Which is when I go about cleaning up, wiping down bottles, or tinkering around on the monitor, randomly pulling up tabs, to create the illusion that I am doing something extremely important... just to extract myself from the last call conversation, that *I* stupidly started on a whim...and... now has everyone screaming at each other...Seriously, I started out talking about Mighty Mouse...

I would much rather the discussions revolve around sports or music. These are the topics that I can actually contribute something substantial to. I'm the girl who knows how many receiving yards the rookie for the Dallas Cowboys has this season, or who Manny Pacquiao is fighting in the upcoming championship bout. From Johnny Rotten to Frank Sinatra, I can babble about music until the wee hours of the morning, thus producing not only better tips, but enough material for arguments that will last for the extent of my shift. And believe it or not, there is nothing sexier than a chick who knows her stuff.

Occasionally, you find yourself sitting next to the guy that talks too much, or you are somehow stuck at the bar (while your friends are battling it out in a deadly session of 'House Of The Dead' in the game room) and being forced to silently watch the mentally incompetent bartender that is struggling to carry on a decent rap session with his customers. You subconsciously make notes on the bright pink Post-Its in your mind, while rolling your eyes, and sipping your beer, just waiting for the moment when he actually pauses long enough to draw a breath, and that's when it happens. The know-it-all, conversationally *superior* snob that usually lurks quietly in the corner of your Temporal Lobe suddenly decides it is time for an impromptu audition for *Who Wants To Be a Millionaire...* Unexpectedly, you hear yourself challenging this person, asking questions that only *you* would know the answer to, and calling him out, on just about everything that he has been boisterously babbling about for the past twenty minutes. Unfortunately for the bar keep, his bored shitless regulars have abruptly sprung to life, cheering you on in your arguments, and laughing loudly as you skewer the poor bastard with pointed words. Always the entertainers, of course, we lords of libations feed off of the energy of the newly revived, that we have accidentally excited, and, in doing our civic duty to protect the noble name of bartenders everywhere, finally slay the clown like imposter with the last devastating blow. Then, ask for the tab, *tip double*, smile, and walk away. This action proves that you aren't a *total* dick. His humiliation became profitable, and you satisfied that nagging voice in the back of your head, the one that incessantly insisted that you, *by any means possible* reduce this jerk ass jester to rubble.

As someone who watches Sports Center everyday and listens to news radio in the car, I have to say that the verbal intercourse being had at the bar nowadays is somewhat *less* than stimulating. I pray for a capable opponent, the worthy adversary. For some reason, these elusive holders of intellectual correspondence would rather be sitting at home, taking bong hits and playing Xbox... This makes me jealous, only because it means that I am stuck at work with the few derelicts that have actually managed to make it through nine straight hours of drinking, and somehow would still like to argue about God, or basketball... When **I** could be *sitting at home*, doing bong hits and playing Xbox...

Chapter Ten
BAD DOODLES AND A BAT PHONE

THAT GUY....

He is bent almost all the way across the bar, trying to coax you into leaning just a *tad* closer so that he can tell you a 'secret'. Breath stinking of cigarettes, booze, and sometimes vomit, tripping over his words, leering at you like a sex offender that has just stumbled upon a super model, alone, in a parking garage...*naked*... These morons take the lead in the race for stupidity.

Somehow, these imbeciles are also completely unaware of how barnyard they are making themselves appear, and further still, they have deluded themselves into thinking that they have an actual shot at scoring with the bartender... wait, retract that, scoring with *anyone*. As soon as he realizes that the bartender is not giving him any play whatsoever, that guy turns to find anyone that will pay attention to him. He's like the Cougar, only way more obnoxious, and toting around a penis to boot.

You know him. He is everywhere. At the office, on the subway, the street corner, the construction site... He is the one whistling at you from three stories up, hollering from the window of a passing car, tossing paper clips at you from the desk in the next cubicle, and in gym class, he is the one lobbing up a volleyball that says "Do you like me..? Check yes or no..." Let me assure you, that even if you check *no*, he will persist anyway, assuming that the dominant male role is in any way appealing to the opposite sex. It is borderline *creeper*, but not completely, because this guy is too dumb to be stalker material.

The loudest person in the room, wearing a fresh wife beater (or one of the newly discovered glittered or *bedazzled* t-shirts) and designer jeans, with spotless sneakers and an impeccable manicure- he is demanding attention and absolutely certain that he is going to get it. What that guy doesn't quite comprehend...is that he is **that guy...**

While there are many different *forms* of **that guy**, the foreordained graceless personality traits that he will radiate are the same. Never having had a serious relationship, for fear of ruining his "player" status, he has no clue how to speak to women, nor does he possess the knowledge enabling him to discern the difference between appropriate and inappropriate comments, conversation, or behavior. Therefore, any self respecting female finds a way to excuse herself from his company. He is then forced to move on to either the innocent twenty one year old that is shooting pool with her also freshly of age girlfriends, or, his only other option...the bar sluts.

Upon first glance, he might seem attractive. This means simply that he has just walked in, you have never seen him before, and he hasn't *spoken* yet. Once he unzips his jacket, unveils the Affliction shirt, reveals the sleeve of trendy tribal tattoos, and saunters over to the bar with his newly purchased Yankees cap twisted ever so slightly to the left, you suddenly turn to the chick working with you and hold up a closed fist, signaling the rock-paper-scissors face off, in hopes that you can possibly win your way out of waiting on him. This self proclaimed ladies' man will toss out several cliché pickup lines even as you are reaching for the coasters, before you have met his eyes, or asked him what he wants to drink. For whatever reason, these retards have come to agree that throwing fifteen lines into the water all at once, is the most *resourceful* way to catch a fish. The old- quality verses quantity law- obviously does *not* apply here. Who knows? Perhaps they are correct. Or, perhaps they have just watched way too many episodes of Jersey Shore.

Sometimes this wonder of modern science is around five feet tall- and what he lacks in height, he makes up for in tasteless etiquette and surly mannerisms. Inexplicably, this guy imagines himself as a sexual superman, even though his reproductive organs are cohesive to those of the graduating class of the local elementary school…and his sexual prowess, is considered… *ahem*…somewhat *jerky*…like hopping on a wooden roller coaster, when you are used to the ultra cool, metal one's. Having fun while aboard this bumpy train is *ultra impossible*, as you spend more time trying to keep your knees from getting banged up and figuring out what the bill for the trip to the Chiropractor is going to cost to set your back right again when it's over. To avoid this displeasing trip to the amusement park altogether, I have coined a phrase that needs no explanation when tossed at the dwarflike creeper…I simply smile, and say; "Sorry honey, you've got to be Six Four to ride this ride…"

Where the younger ones are concerned, it is hard not to feel bad for him. You know in your heart that in five years, he is going to come across a picture of himself, and say "Damn, I looked like a real jackass, why didn't anyone tell me…?" Therefore, I try to catch them early, and insult them as much as possible, in hopes of snapping them out of the current MTV induced dementia that has taken hold of their subconscious, the enveloping Lil Wayne phenomena that is somehow forcing them to fist bump instead of handshake, or buy the new Eminem album instead of The Bouncing Souls collection that was recently released on vinyl..

To reach **That Guy** status, you must endure a very demanding schedule and an intricately planned routine- (Unbeknownst to any skateboarder, snowboarder, or lacrosse player) Consisting of, but not limited to, these daily tasks include; Going to the gym, tanning, shopping, ironing clothes, getting manicures, pedicures and massages, hanging out for more than five minutes a *year* at GNC, going to the salon, designating a washcloth *and* toothbrush for cleaning tennis shoes, mixing up protein shakes, dividing up dietary supplements, and wasting an average of thirty dollars a week on hair gel. Outside of shopping, and an occasional mani-pedi session with the girlfriends, I wouldn't do *one* of these things, unless forced by gun point...and *I* have a vagina...

It is hilarious to watch this guy in action, because even if he is on the other side of the room, you can *still* almost hear the atrocities that are coming out of his mouth, smell the bad cologne, and see the pack of Newport's falling out of his pocket. The laughingstock of every normal guy in the bar, he somehow mistakes the attention for popularity, and decides that karaoke would be a good idea. This is the moment when the bartenders begin pouring themselves a drink and then wait patiently for the show. After cheers-ing, everyone's focus becomes directed toward the stage, where **that guy** is about to put on what he thinks is a once in a lifetime performance, of Ice Ice Baby...

When it comes to **that guy**, nothing is off limits. He will order a hundred dollars worth of Jager bombs, slip out to his SUV every half hour to do lines of coke off of the center console, grab a pile of fifties out of his pocket to pay for breakfast, and invite everyone in the bar back to his plush palace for an after party. With bar sluts on either arm, he will feel like a King, act like a teenager, and annoyingly nudge your arm every four seconds, insinuating that you should laugh at the unfunny comment that he has repeated twelve times in a row, in the worst attempt at replica ghetto slang ever recorded.

Another thing that **that guy** forgets is something that the rest of us know full well; your business does *not* need to be spread all over the street. People that care about their reputation, don't go broadcasting personal information around town just to gain social status. The guys with multiple phones, blue tooth earpieces, or palm pilots, are usually drug dealers, bookies, scumbag lawyers, or, are cheating on their wives, and in no way do they want *anyone* to know that it is a different phone than the one they were using just seconds prior. So, that guy, who 'accidentally' informs everyone that he has a 'secret' phone (that he has no qualms about pulling out, and answering, loudly, in front of *everyone* that he just met) is just trying to show off the fact that he has a secondary phone...what a goon...I mean, wasn't the bat phone only used for stealthy information passing between Batman and Commissioner Gordon..? Oh, that had to be before this guys' time...Or he had Batman mixed up with that *other* cartoon, what was it...The Ambiguously Gay Duo...? Let me describe for you a guy that used to come into my bar. He wasn't bad looking, kind of a meathead though, and muscles aren't really my thing. Anyway, he was older, about forty or so, and he had a wife and they had five kids. They were rich, but they were redneck rich, so while you would normally be jealous of the diamonds and the Range Rovers, you kinda feel better knowing that they are rednecks, so it doesn't really count. When he bought a Viper, he came to the bar to show everyone, and while he was there, he showed me a set of keys and a tiny phone. Not really 'in tune' with the hip new ways to cheat on your spouse, I asked "Uh...what's that for?"

"It's my Bat Phone, and the keys to my Bat Cave." He smirked.

So I sat and listened to him explain how when he gets a call from one of his girlfriends, (can you believe he said *one* of his girlfriends...?) he has to be able to meet her somewhere, and he had to have a place to take chicks when he was leaving the bar, so he was renting an apartment in the neighborhood. He had a fully furnished, pimped out bat cave. One of my girlfriends says she was there one night; she *then* swore to her fiancée that she didn't put on the cat woman suit and bang the meathead redneck in his stupid secret man cave. Every time I saw him after that he would smile knowingly over his wife's shoulder, winking suggestively and jingling keys in his pocket. A few months later, I ran into him at the mall, asked about his wife and he told me that they were separated. After a few minutes of conversation, I learned that he was in Dallas 'on business' when his *wife* called his *bat phone*, which she wasn't supposed to have the number to, and when he answered, she informed him that she was standing in his hidden lair, and that she wanted a divorce. I assumed that he was too busy getting numbers to store in his new electronic 'black book' and way more concerned with scraping used rubbers off of the floor in his dirty den of sordidness to realize one enormous

MAJORLY IMPORTANT detail...***His wife received the bank statements.*** He is ***that guy.*** An older, out of stock model, but still on the lot. I bet his sons grow up to be mini-that guy's too.

Those guys are always looking for an easy 'in' for conversation. They will notice every single detail about you, just so they can assume that they are the only one who's ever noticed it before. Thank you, asshole, but my boyfriend tells me I have nice eyes all the time. No thanks, I don't want to see your back tattoos just because you notice one on my wrist. And, I like my earrings too, douche bag, that's why I bought them.

I recently went to a bar with one of my best friends, and there was this guy who was blatantly staring at her, all night long. Of course he was pulling out all the stops, hovering nearby, trying to snake a bar stool that opened up next to her, just your normal run-of-the-mill-*that-guy* behavior. We even had the guys that were with us tell him to beat it; and form the protective guy barrier around us. I noticed that he was wearing a wedding ring so I was completely grossed out. Last call arrived, and on our way out of the bar, the pig was sitting out front, waiting. He called something out to her as we passed, so I turned around and said "Why don't you go home to your wife, douche." As we climbed into her car, he walked over, yet he didn't attempt to talk to us through the window. I looked in the passenger side mirror, and saw that he was leaning up against the door to her gas tank. "Oh my God, he's pissing on the car!" I yelled. She started freaking out, so I hopped out and decked him in the mouth. He then started swinging on me, like a complete lunatic. Fortunately, he missed my face and planted one right in my shoulder. That's when one of the guys with us chased him across the parking lot. Just one more shining example of douche-ism. That guy was pissed that he got turned down, and decided to empty his bladder on her rear quarter panel. What a loser.

For the ones who *should* know better, it is a different story. When you are past the age of twenty five, a little light bulb should have at least *flickered* above your head in the reflection of that mirror that you check every eight seconds… If that moment has gone unnoticed by you, I advise that you take a few moments from your eventful day of cruising around in your souped up Escalade, and rent the movie *Whiteboys*. Upon reviewing this film, if you do not see the main characters as totally unbalanced, then sadly, you are lost causes my friends. There is no saving you, and you will remain an asshole, **forever.**

Chapter Eleven
"WHO ORDERED THE GRATUITY..?"

An Awesomely Bad Collection of Word Vomit...

Every once in a while, this job has moments that make you laugh the mascara right off of your face. Beat red, crying, snorting, and dangerously close to a little pee coming out, you somehow, someway, manage to pull it together long enough to reiterate the verbal crime just committed, to the rest of the sufferers... but, usually, it is just you...all alone...just sober enough to bite your tongue, yet, one shot too many over the ability to control your wit... dancing on the precipice of saying something *so* mean, that your tip goes flying out the window and a fight is inevitable. But, usually, it's too funny to actually give a shit. Sometimes these moments are picked up on by innocent bystanders, but not fully appreciated by anyone other than the bartenders. Allow me to give some examples of the retarded remarks, frequently asked stupid questions, and downright *ludicrous* statements and that I have witnessed over the years.

A waitress walked over to greet a couple and their child, who had grabbed a booth for happy hour... approaching the table, she informed them that we had a fabulous crab dip, and that the soup of the day was Clam Chowder. Sparking an interest by the client, the clam craving subject then asked the waitress, "Really? What kind..?" Meaning Red or White, and in a dumbstruck moment, the waitress simply responded "I believe its Campbell's..." And walked away.

This one is my favorite. I was working in a fine dining restaurant, (White table cloths and everything...) I had a man order the Prime Rib dinner. I asked how he would like it cooked, asked for the side item preferences, and went on my merry way. Of course, the merriment took a hard left turn when I arrived tableside with his meal, and, as I placed his plate in front of him, watched his face change from pleased to pissed. "Hey, where're my ribs at..?" He asked. That fact that he was *serious* in his inquiry is what makes this story so funny. Mustering ever bit of self-containment that I could possibly be expected to, stifling the guffaw that was threatening to break free, I replied, "Well, you see sir, Prime Rib is a *steak...*"

Another one of my favorites is when people ask if you *have* a bathroom, instead of simply asking where it is. I usually say "No, you have to go outside." And watch as they uncomfortably try to figure out where they are going to relieve themselves. The joke is mostly funny, until the too-drunk redneck unzips, and reaches for a pint glass...

Another good one. At my bar we have around twenty beers on tap. The taps are not hidden in a secret room, underneath the floor boards. They are sitting directly *on* the bar, in plain view. In fact, depending on where you stand, you might actually have to look *over* the tap handles to see me, and yet you still say..."Hey, what do you have on draft..?" Watch out dude...you suddenly have an ashtray flying at your head...

"I'll take a Bud heavy."
"A what?"
"A Bud heavy."
"And what the hell is that?"
"You know, *not* Bud Light..."
"You mean a *Budweiser...*"
"Yeah."
FUCK YOU. GO SUCK SOMEPLACE ELSE.

One of the most annoying things *ever*, and it would blow your mind how often it happens. "Can I get a ten, a five, and five ones?" As they hand me a twenty. Just say **change** you jackass. I can count. And *because* you felt it necessary to explain it to me, now you are getting two fives, eight ones, four quarters and two rolls of pennies. Have fun putting *that* in the cigarette machine.

Time for a brilliant observation yet? In the nightclub..."It's really loud in here... can you maybe ask if they can turn it down...?"

A girl once studied the 'specials' menu, with a very strange and curious look on her face. Then she asked me what "rain" drinks were. It took me a minute, but then I looked at her and said, "You mean *rail*..?"

"How much are the three dollar rail drinks..?" Really? You just one the medal.

"What's in a whiskey sour?" Lord give me strength.

"Do you have water here?" Lol. **Nope**.

"Does *Bud* mean Budweiser...?" (That one was from a *waitress*.)

"Can I get a Strong Island..?" By the way, if you are the one doing this, you need to be shot. And...*hello*...Can I get a **tip**..?

"How old do you have to be to get in?"
"Twenty one."
"Ya'll be checkin ID's...?"

One more. The phone rings. "Hey...are you open...?" Hmmm... let me think... did someone just answer the *fucking phone*..?!?!

"Can I get a Club sandwich, on white, with no Ham, no American, no Swiss, and no turkey..?" So...you want a BLT... just ask for a fucking BLT, Stupid.

"I'll take a yin-yang."
"You mean a Yuengling?"

"What's the difference between a bottle and a draft..?"
"Well, one has a Penis and the other has a Vagina…"

"I need a Tequlia Sunrise…more tequila than sunrise…"

"I want something strong…"
"Uh….like…?"
"I guess…a…Budweiser…"

"What's your poison…?
"Methamphetamine."
"Well….. shit….I've got Red Bull……?"

"Scu me..." Ugh. This is the worst. You find yourself turning around and asking why they can't find the strength to just put that extra S in there. 'Scuse me…or maybe even the added syllable. *Ex*-cuse me…How fucking hard is that..? Fuck.

"Six-fifty."
"But I know the owner."
"Me fucking too. Now give me six fucking fifty before I rip your fucking head off."

"Can I get a coke-soda."

"Can I get cheese on that gratuity…and a to-go box..?"
When adding gratuity to a check, you must be prepared for the repercussions. Such as, the bafflement that appears in the voices and on the faces of those who have just received the tab... "*What's Gravity*

doing on our check...?"... and... *"Why does gravy cost so much...?"* ..." *We might have to split this gratuity...did it come with fries...?"* Or better yet...."*Did anyone get a Gyro..? ...A **Gyro**?* Really...? We aren't in *Greece* dumbass, that's the included **tip**. Seriously... and you people *genuinely* wonder why we add it on there...

Chapter Twelve
"THAT'S NOT A CROUTON, IT'S A BREADCRUMB"...

The Customer is always...annoying as hell

That saying, *the customer is always right*...a more bullshit statement has never been invented. This monstrosity *had* to have been made up by a *customer*, before catching on and running rampant like some deadly virus. Seriously, have you ever heard anyone other than a bitching customer speak those arrogant words..? Unless it was an assistant manager at a shitty corporate chain- berating the fifteen year old hostess for sighing in frustration at the couple that keeps changing tables- who *truly* believes this ill-conceived notion, no respectable bartender, server, hostess, or fucking dishwasher would be caught dead even whispering this phrase in their *sleep*.

Years of experience have trained me to have a more highly expressive opinion, and, believe me; it has nothing to do with any of the *others* being **right**. As a matter of fact, you know the **first** way we can tell that you are wrong..? *You walk in.*

Get it..? Yeah, well, even if you *think* you get it, you really fucking don't. Check this out...I have had more people complain about me, than ticks on a stray dog that is found roaming through the woods in West Virginia...

There are a thousand different personality traits that will clash off the bat. There are a hundred similar signals that first-encounter body language manages to convey, louder than *any* voice that happens to be taking over the room. There are a dozen ways to glare at someone without *actually* glaring. And there are a few particular ways to piss someone off to the point where a life sentence doesn't seem that bad...***But***, there is only **one** way to decide that *hate* is dominating the situation. And that way is confrontation.

A bone is only a bone, until two lions decide that only **one** *of them is going to walk away with it...*

For some insane reason, people like to fight. If they aren't fighting, they would like to at least *partake* in a good-ol'-fashioned witch burning... Maybe the lynch mob will attempt at an incredulous invasion, and God willing, tie a metaphorical rope around my neck... In all honesty, I punch people way too quick and *way* too often to even be *in* this precarious predicament...But I find myself caught up in the mayhem anyway.

Customer complaints are infamous for being exaggerated and overly picky. The majority of people are just looking for something for free, and they figure that the easiest way to accomplish this is by complaining about what they got. Never mind that they ordered it, ate it, drank it, *loved it,* all while being completely content...until they decide that it might have cost too much for them to afford dessert..

Most of the time, the managers cater to the desires of these whining wonders of society, and either comp their *entire* check, or, return from the office with coupons for free meals, desserts, and specialty drinks. To the server, this is the insult of all insults, and we spend the remainder of the evening figuring out away to send a Morse coded message to the kitchen, prompting the chef to insert one of his body parts into the brownie sundae that is being prepared for this disgruntled guest.

I am not saying that there aren't admissible reasons for a complaint. I too, have complained about my waitress. You know, *her*...the one that is standing in the corner texting, instead of refilling my glass that has stood empty on the table for a half an hour, in front of my undercooked burger that arrived with a side order of French fries, *instead* of the Caesar salad that I asked for. This is a problem, and must be rectified. No doubt about it. Although those of us who serve in this army try to bypass throwing another soldier under the bus whenever possible, sometimes it is just plain unavoidable. And shitty service is a green light for waving over a manger, listing the citations in a calm yet condescending tone, while shooting *hahaha* glances at the waitress, who finally got off the damn phone.

Now, there are *way* more comical complaints than legitimate ones. For example, griping about the misspelled Mesclun salad printed on the menu, for fear of your six year old child reading that 'Mescaline' is being served up in heavy doses…This is a tad ridiculous, and falls under the 'outré objection' section of *The Complainers Guide to Doomed Dining*. By the way, if your child knows what Mescaline is…you've got bigger problems than proper grammar…

Also, complaining about things that *aren't* on the menu, is even worse. *"Damn, ya'll don't have wings…?"* For obvious reasons, this makes you look, well, retarded. How can you possibly be so bored, that you invent things to bitch about?

My favorite of the customer grievances? The ones that are so farfetched and hilarious, that keeping a straight face or not shooting a remark that is literally dripping with sarcasm, becomes *impossible*.

Example. I recently had a couple walk into the bar at five minutes to eight. They sat down and peered at the taps.
"Oooo, I will have a Fosters." The woman said.
"And I will take an MGD." The man ordered.
After drawing the requested drafts, I set them on the designated coasters and said "Seven dollars."
"Excuse me..?" The woman asked, immediately fixing her gaze on the specials' board behind the bar that read; Happy Hour 3-8pm. $2.00 Domestic Drafts. $3.00 rail drinks.
"Seven dollars." I repeated.
"No, it says two dollar domestic drafts." She accused, pointing at the sign.
"Yes, it does. But Fosters is an import, not a domestic. Therefore, it is seven dollars."

"But we have five minutes left."

"No, it's not a Happy Hour special."

"But, it says two dollar domestic drafts until eight o'clock."

"Yes, I am aware of the signs and the specials. *But*, Fosters is NOT a domestic beer."

"Well, you didn't tell me that." The woman glared.

"Well, you didn't ask." At this point, I settle into position for the argument that is going to ensue as the result of someone else's stupidity.

"Right, but you didn't bother to tell me that Fosters isn't a Happy Hour beer special."

"Right, but you didn't bother to ask."

"Well, I don't want it then."

Sigh. This always happens. I guess I am supposed to assume that every single person that sits down at the bar needs me to describe the basic rules of Happy Hour, or hold their hand while explaining the difference between imported and domestic beer. Here is a helpful hint, if it says *Imported from Australia* on the tap; chances are it wasn't made in Milwaukee.

"Well, you ordered it, and I made it, so…"

"I need to speak with your manager."

Ugh. The Deftones song '*7 words*' was actually written about these, the seven dreaded words of the industry.

"He's in a meeting."

"I need to speak with your manager."

"*He's in a meeting.*"

"What, you can't interrupt?"

"Nope."

This is the moment that I choose to walk away. Before I completely lose it and grab a bottle of Captain and smash it over her head, then use the remnants to slit her husbands' throat for just *sitting there*, wordlessly watching instead of slapping her with a fucking muzzle, and telling her to just shut up and drink the God damned beer. I watch as this woman gets up, and begins roaming around aimlessly until she stumbles upon the manager meeting that is being held quietly in a far off corner of the room. I continue to observe this escaped demon, as she dramatically paints a story board for the GM, waving her arms and lying through her teeth. Trust me when I say that, tonight, I will be on my knees, bedside, hands folded, staring at the ceiling and praying that she gets hit by a bus. Thankfully, my manager directed her to a section that is not expected to be waited on by the bartenders, and let the UFC training waiter deal with her. I felt a tiny bit bad for him, until he told me that he dunked his, um, under carriage, in her butter, just moments before delivering the shrimp platter to her table.

One of my absolute favorite things that people say is; "I know I'm being a pain in the ass, but…" then their voice trails off and they glance away, waiting for you to say "oh no, don't worry about it." I never grant them that satisfaction. Step one is acknowledging that you are aware of the fact that you are being a pain in the ass…step two is actually doing something about it. So… (trailing off…)

Another hindering situation is the one where the customer attempts to get a free drink by leaving a sip, literally a *sip*, in their glass, and disappearing for fifteen minutes, only to return and demand to know what happened to their drink. This is one of the most harebrained decisions of *all time*. It's not our first barbeque honey. You have to get up pretty early in the morning to pull a fast one on us, we are professionals. Like we didn't know that the glass was empty, right? In fact, it is *so* stupid, that it even becomes comical to the bar back. Let's face it…if the *bar back* is pointing at you and saying, "*Dude….*" It's time to just sack up, and order another drink… 'Cause you aren't fooling *anyone*…

This colorful illustration is just one, out of two-thousand-seven-hundred-and-thirty- four instances of bullshit bellyaching that I have been subjected to over the years, and the counter continues to spin. Endlessly logging, relentlessly recording, and gathering dramatic data to not only support, but *confirm* the fact that customers are indeed, the **bane** of our existence. Especially when they are armed with withering glances and dirty dispositions…

Chapter Thirteen
HEY MISTER DEEJAY

Side One Track One...

Music is the key to a good time, no matter what the situation. A road trip, a casual evening at home, a first kiss moment, and yes, the gathering at the bar. If the deejay is spinning 80's classics, and everyone in the bar is feeling it, dancing wildly, and emptying out their 401k's, just to keep the good vibes flowing, then you can classify it as a fantastic evening. If you just *can't* find a way to drag your friends off of the dance floor, and the only pause that you can force yourself to take from tearing up the planks, is the undeniable urge that Mother Nature plants in your urethra... then, it is also, a *fabulous* night.

But, there is always a way to destroy the fun, and it just so happens that the Maestro holds the key to Pandora's box. One bad song or remix, and suddenly the dance floor becomes a riotous mob, an angry collection of prettied up prima donnas, catty cougars, and bitter boyfriends (the ones that were *finally* getting down with the dice throwing move). If the bad becomes worse, the turntables will become responsible for the poisonous gas that is being released upon the sweaty crowd, and the strobe lights are instantly the full moon that suddenly brings out the werewolves. Transforming the once rhythmical congregation into a messy assortment of cranky complainers, drunken jerkoff's, and desperate dancers, that are visibly *yearning* for a release from their tumultuous daily grind.

Basically, being the guy in the booth carries with it a more tedious responsibility than *any* other job on the face of the planet... Because...they hold in their hand the key to everyone else's good time. *So* glad I am just a lowly bartender -Although, I will be the first to admit, that the deejay is the one guy who is awesomely cool, without actually aspiring to *be* cool. He is the guy who drinks his face off, pulls more chicks than any other guy in the bar, has the hot girlfriend, and everyone knows his name. Basically he is the exact *opposite* of That Guy.

The bartender-deejay alliance is unlike any other. Above and beyond the kinship of siblings, bigger than the benevolence of best friends, far superior to the *fellowship of the ring*...There is an unspoken bond between the deejay and his bartender. One reason for this relation is the quiet understanding that they share, *knowing* that they are the superiors in every room. If not for them, no one would be dancing *or* drinking, and the party would be as arousing as a quilt making extravaganza at grandma's house. The musical master is always looking out for the ones who supply his booze, which is of course, the only thing that drags him out of bed every afternoon. The deejay is the coolest guy in every room, and when the party is becoming too much for the drink slinging diva's, he throws on their favorite song, bringing their spirits up and preventing them from channeling **Carrie**, therefore, saving everyone in the club from being incinerated.

On the nights when there is no Mad Hatter scratching the vinyl, the jukebox is the Lord of all creation. The newer jukeboxes can either light up your life, or make you want to stab yourself in the eye. The fancier ones now house a button, *play next*. This magical extra allows you to skip your song to the front of the list, for a nominal fee. It seems nothing short of *miraculous*, when scooting your Face to Face track ahead of the thirteen people that have played the new Jay Z monstrosity, and all is right with the world when you can dominate the surrounding atmosphere by playing the entire Adrenaline album before anyone else can slip a five into the seductive slot of the computerized disc jockey. Unfortunately, all coins have two sides. The dream becomes a nightmare when you realize that you have been bullied off the jukebox, when Justin Timberlake's latest track comes swirling over the airways, invading your brain and causing you to peek your head around the corner, finding that two girls decked out from head to toe in Charlotte Russe, toting Coach bags, and sporting stilettos, with a fistful of dollar bills and sipping Apple Martini's, are robotically scrolling through the top-forty list. *This will ruin your evening.* So much for the Chino marathon that you were enjoying with your boys, you are now fatefully subjected to the mainstream melodies that have subliminally taken over the minds of the *others.*

An eclectic mix of music is necessary however, to prevent the patrons from doing to the bar what heavy metal bands did to hotel rooms in the early nineties, and only the *finest* of deejay's can accomplish this feat. Spinning a wondrous variety of tunes, dodging the requests of the musically retarded, and even in the worst of situations, keeping the majority of the room happy and dancing with his carefully crafted opus. Even while sweating his way through a brutal hangover, this orchestratic genius has artfully honed the ability to deter the boob flashing groupies and request mongers, miraculously managed to keep his girlfriend from strangling someone, pose suavely for the website-camera-guy, and get completely wasted all in one night. Every night. Being a deejay takes a lot of willpower, a ton of work, and respectably, more knowledge than it takes to be one of those brain surgeon guys that I keep hearing so much about. So cheers to you, Mister Deejay. Thanks for keeping the party going.

Chapter Fourteen
PLAUSABLE DENIABILITY

*"No, that was **last** week, and I was off..."*

Seeing as how the eighty-six board is *never* completely accurate, and the managers never have a clue what the soup of the day is, or whether or not we actually *have* Grey Goose, there are a few times during the course of your evening that you might find yourself caught up in an embarrassing moment. Looking like you have no idea what you are talking about, sheepishly having to tell someone that the awesome fish dinner that you were describing was *yesterdays* special, and begging your work counterpart to take the table to which you just *assured* that the lemonade was freshly squeezed...even though you saw the carton of Minute Maid.. These are *all* things that happen every day, in The Life.

These moments can render you incapacitated, after all, nobody likes looking foolish. But, the tricks of the trade prevail, keeping your ego intact, and the customers unaware of any inside confusion. Here are some of the ways that we dance around the fact that we fucked up.

We like to pawn off responsibility whenever possible, and if we can blame *anyone* else for the current predicament, believe me, we are going to. So, if you ordered cheese sticks, and twenty five minutes go by, and you start shouting about the melty mozzarella that you haven't received yet, watch out, we are going to brain wash you into thinking that you never actually ordered it, that it was simply a figment of your super hungry imagination.

Or we hit you with the slider. "Oh, that must have been with the *other* bartender, let me check on that for you." This is when we haul ass to the kitchen, screaming that we need an order of fried cheese on the fly, and then return to you, apologizing for any inconvenience, citing that the kitchen lost the ticket, and offering to comp the appetizer for you. See how we avoided admitting that we just plain forgot…? Don't get huffy, *everybody* does this at least twice a day.

How about when the specials board entices you to order a four dollar Hieneken, and then the bartender charges you five-fifty, going completely unnoticed by you for the first five rounds. This is not because the bartender doesn't know about the special, it is because we are trying to weasel an extra dollar-fifty out of *you,* and into our tip bucket. Until you actually call us out on it, we will do this to you for hours on end, pretending that we have no idea, insisting that we are just going by normal Friday night pricing.

Another way to lose you in the shuffle, is to pretend that we have absolutely *no* idea what you are talking about. Say you have a credit card charge that has a somewhat 'questionable' tip on it. Just know that I am thirty dollars richer, and there is absolutely no way that you are seeing that cash *ever* again. Unless you have live footage of yourself signing your receipt, there is no way to prove that you didn't actually leave that gracious gratuity. Basically, what it boils down to is this, you tried to stiff your bartender, and they took matters into their own hands. And because you handed over your credit card, in a drunken stupor, you are now liable for the tip that you should have left in the first place. As much tracking as one can do, calling every day for two weeks, retracing steps and consulting friends, it is unlikely that the reimbursement of this cash will ever appear in your bank statement, so just let it go.

What's even funnier, is when there are allergies involved. If you are allergic to mushrooms, and somehow a mushroom winds up in your salad, it will never in a *thousand years* be your **server's** fault.

"Oh my god, I wrote it on the ticket *twice, and* I went in and told the Chef *myself.* I'm so sorry, I'll get a manager." This is a bold faced lie. The server really couldn't have cared less, blamed it on the kitchen, and lied about getting a manager. You won't see a manager for the rest of the night, because even if you ask the busboy to find one, the waitress has already slipped him an extra twenty, a bag of weed, or a promissory note for a blow job…So, short of you standing up and screaming at the top of your lungs, which you probably can't do due to the allergic reaction that your body is having, you might as well ask for a doggy bag for the bread and appetizer, and have your date run you to the emergency room real quick.

Pretending that I am unaware of the things that are sabotaging your evening is not a talent that everyone possesses, and, I must say, is quite the acquired skill. I might just post it on my resume', if ever I decide to leave the family that I currently reside with. Playing stupid to customer complaints is just another perk of the job, and I continue to hone my mastery, proving that sleight of hand just might win out over arguing, simply by the demeanor in which you practice. If the customer is so **irate**, that my calm, collected voice encourages his rage, it only appears to others that he has just had *one* too many cocktails to carry on a civilized conversation, further fueling my point for legitimacy…especially when the client becomes so flustered by my professionalism that he starts dropping the F bomb, and disturbing the dining pleasure of the other buyers…. Killing them with kindness is like handing them a shot of TNT, and it works *every* time..

When confronted with a "Hey, let me ask you…Were you working the other night when Sheila jumped across the bar at that girl…?" situation, well, *this* is unstable terrain. You know they have already checked the schedule- and that it is quite possible that they have you on camera slipping your fingers into a set of brass knuckles and screaming "Let's do this bitch!" But, that little voice inside of you tells you to just look at your boss with wide eyes and say, "Nope, Daisy and I switched shifts that night." And then turn around and pretend to clean something until your manager walks away, scratching his head. Deny it all, right to the end.

Lying about who did what, losing the tab, and 'forgetting' where you were when a crazy instance involving a friend-slash-co-worker took place, are also accrued to the personality traits that not everyone in this industry can readily wrap their mind around, so *assuming* that your accomplices were also granted these attributes is a tricky business. When expecting one of your esteemed associates to know *why* you are winking, it is imperative to revive your memory, and conjure up the conversation that you had at two in the morning, after a long night of boozing, and recall whether or not you *actually* filled them in-even half heartedly-two days ago, on what they were supposed to 'conveniently' forget, while laughing about the law suit that she has just accidentally involved you in, by threatening that one girl who used to date her cousins best friend...remember...?

It's a lot to take in, I know. But keep reading. In the most peculiar of circumstances, the manager happens to be the one that has to work the most word magic. Really, it all comes down to one thing...whether or not we are ever going to see you again. If the manager gets the vibe that you are, indeed, going to return, he will spare no expense at reinstating your happiness. That includes lumping every one of his servers into a collective heap, chalking them all up as moronic charity cases, and promising that at least half of them will *not* have a job tomorrow. This is all bullshit of course, and while the reprimanding will be vicious, we will continue on in this defective outfit, until someone fucks up so bad, that they are now a liability, and are cut loose. Politics, politics. Basically what I'm trying to say is that you are screwed, and you might as well accept it. Because you really don't need to exert that kind of energy, just to be told in a hundred different ways, "You know, I wasn't here that night, and I just don't know what to tell ya..."

Chapter Fifteen
JAGER MUSCLES AND BEER GOGGLE LASER SURGERY

"Knowing when to say when..."

Sigh. Not everyone understands that there *is* a time to ask for the tab and get away from other humans, before starting a fight or ending up in a gnaw-your-arm-off-in-the- morning situation. Enhanced meathead muscles are not comically injected into an unsuspecting grocery store clerk that is stepping off of an elevator (for those of you who aren't movie buffs; that was an *Innerspace* reference...) and they aren't obtained by sitting in the corner, timidly sipping on an amaretto sour... No, no...They are earned by full on face-fucking a bottle of brown, licorice flavored devils blood...more commonly referred to as...*Jagermeister.*

This fiendish fluid will without question, incapacitate your ability to call it quits, *almost* as quickly as it will spur on a dick measuring contest that *always* ends up in a bloody bar brawl (which can be viewed two million times a day on YouTube.) Forewarning the *idiots*, incase you were unaware... almost as soon as you order the Jager, the bartenders are putting out an APP. (Translation: a professional premonition that there will be a scuffle.) It is inevitable. It is also imbedded in the German translation of the word *Jagermeister* ; The Deer Hunter. *Deer hunter*... Um... didn't they make a movie called *The Deer Hunter..*? If I recall correctly, it was a movie about blood and war and it ended when you felt so shitty, that you had to turn it off, or risk tossing yourself out of a window.

Jager muscles are known to suddenly overcome the one who is normally the more subdued one of the group. One minute he is smiling and dancing, a second later he is flipping over tables and challenging anyone in the building to a drinking contest or an arm wrestling match. Unnatural strength and superhero powers will most likely accompany this outrageous display of manhood, which can be controlled *solely* by the one person in the room who can actually talk some sense into this steroid-ridden subject...the *bartender*. The bartender is also known as the referee. We might not always wear the stripes, but we definitely carry the whistle. Vaulting over the bar as if we are an Olympian on a Gold Medal hurdle run, we intervene quicker than you can even turn to find a doorman. Shoving our arms in between this Pee Wee Herman gone Grizzly and whoever his foe might be, we remind him peacefully, yet sternly, that he is dangerously close to being kicked out. Periodically we succeed, but, more commonly we find ourselves canoeing into the rapids of Testosterone. This is the moment when all you can do as the supplier of ire-inducing inebriants is jump ship, and let the bouncers have their fun, by jamming an oar up his ass, and tossing the disrupter of fun out into the snow. If he so happens to scratch his face along the pavement on his way...well, that is just an added bonus.

Those on the other side of the drunken fence, are less worried about fighting and more concerned with getting laid. Unfortunately, these guys are way past the point of high standards. Or even mediocre standards. Or *standards*, for that matter. Their hooch hampered irises are crippling their ability to discern the difference between pretty, pretty fucked up, and pretty ugly. *We* are unable at this point to steer them in a direction that won't end up in devastation. After two or three attempts to rescue our fellow boozers, we must accept defeat, untie the apron strings, and send them on their way to Hell's kitchen. Blame us if you will, but remember, *you* were the one in the trance, following the demonic whistle of the teapot...

Beer goggles are collectively worn by the bulk of the bar after eleven o'clock. It's like that movie; *The Happening.* You might be able to see it coming, but, the scenario usually ends up the same. Instead of running for the subway, you unwillingly become a spectator in the depraved sport of All Pro Intoxicated Shepherds; herding animals up the ramp into the slaughterhouse… randomly selecting equally intoxicated ewes to share in their evening of sin… What the shepherds fail to realize, is that they are going to wake up in the **barn** in the morning, scratching their beards, wondering what the bah-ing noise ringing in their ears' is, and wondering why their genitals itch…

My advice to the guzzlers who know they will be gorging themselves on Jager for the evening? A chaperone. When relying on the buddy-system, you can rest easy knowing that your wingman will not allow you to make any bad decisions regarding your private area. And, if for some reason your custodian fails to prevent the unthinkable from taking place, at least you have someone to dump the blame on, and share the humiliation with.

Chapter Sixteen
SERVERS GONE SHITTY

"Forget the Good...Give me the bad, the worse, and the ugly..."

For some inexplicable reason, the people that spend their days waiting on others, hand and foot, *actually* decide that going "out" would somehow be a good idea. We might as well walk the plank. In fact, we pretty much resign ourselves to dumpster duty as soon as we step foot into a bar, restaurant, or seven-eleven. It's almost as if we have blinking neon over our head that says "Go ahead, shit in my pancakes...I will tip double just because I know about the pain that is throbbing in your ankle right now..."
(To be honest, that is *only* for the elder ladies that are waiting on us at breakfast, *after* we have been out boozing like our life depended on it. I mean, these bitches used to be *us*...)

What this chapter is *really* about is the ones who just flat out suck. You know the one's I'm talking about. Those incapable idiots that somehow landed a job, even though they don't know the difference between veal and lamb chops... The ones that recite the specials while staring at the notes that they have scribbled on their hand in blue Sharpie...The ones who couldn't tell you whether or not it is Jell-o or crème brulee..

Put it to you this way, when I ask what kind of fish is the catch of the day, you'd better fucking know...*Or*, if I want to know what the soup de jour is, don't you dare say "let me check…" you'd better know what medium rare means, you'd better bring me water with *no* lemon in it, and you'd better stay on top of my empty wine glass…

The screening process for good servers these days is undoubtedly being conducted by Ben Stein, being proven over and over by the ever present ho-hum look…the monotone spiel that they spout off, not really caring whether or not anyone is listening, they are going to forget your appetizer, screw up your side orders, and serve you an undercooked steak *every* time, all the while knowing that they are going to add gratuity to your check and disappear so that you can't dispute it.

It seems that wearing this 'Hello, my name is Bartender' sticker is a prerequisite for shitty service when dining out. I mean it when I say that the Rookies have set up shop in a training course, in every restaurant on Earth, and those trained by the Rookies, have a specific agenda…To make those in this business suffer every disappointment known to man, when attempting to venture outside of the familiarity that is their home base of operations. Think about it. If you work at a law firm, and you suddenly find yourself in a pickle, needing immediate representation, you aren't going to flip through the Yellow pages and seek outside council. If your father is a mechanic, you are not getting your oil changed or your carburetor looked at by Joe Shmoe in the shop down the street. The same goes for the cocktailer that is scouting out an exhilarating new location for nightlife. We rarely step outside of the comfort zone of our own bars, for quite a few reasons. By definition, we are regulars. No matter which side of the bar we happen to be residing on at the moment, we have logged the man hours required to gain the recognition that we deserve. Not wanting to miss out on our fun, by braving out beyond the boundaries that we have grown accustomed to, most of us prefer to remain where we *know* our good time will not be destroyed by the attitude of a disgruntled bartender.

The situation becomes far worse when you meet a friend for lunch, settle into a gossip session, and find yourself being waited on by Leather Face. Trying not to stare, preoccupying your mind by studying the menu, you order an Iced Tea without looking up. You spend the next few minutes wondering how you are ever going to be comfortable eating food that was carried to your table by the ghastly gorilla that has a face mangled by Shingles, dirt under her finger nails, and unidentifiable stains caked on her apron. This is the moment when you toss a five dollar bill on the table, run out giggling, and sigh with relief once safely out of distance, thankful that you didn't even stay long enough to sip that green-glowing glass of iced tea. I mean, I *love* eating out, and finding new places to take my friends, *but*, if Shrek is cooking my food and the troll things that live under the bridge in *Willow* are delivering it to my table, *I'm the fuck outta there.*

Chapter Seventeen
HAPPY HOLIDAYS...

Every bartender knows which dates to tell their friends that they just can't make it...Those dates are as follows, starting at the beginning of the calendar. New Years Eve, Valentine's Day, Saint Patty's day, Mothers Day, Memorial Day weekend, Fathers Day, Fourth of July weekend, Labor Day weekend, Halloween, The night before Thanksgiving, Black Friday, and Christmas Eve. Strangely, people dread being with their family *that* much, that the latter holidays are traditionally the *biggest* drinking days of the year. What sucks for the rest of us, is, we aren't really ever concerned with the loot, we just want to be on the other side, for once, partaking in the festivities, maybe throwing dust to the wind and having ourselves an off-the-reservation type of evening too.

Valentine's Day is the goofiest thing ever created. Basically, a bunch of *un*romantic couples making reservations, dressing up, and shaving things that they haven't shaved in **months**, in preparation for the *one* day a year that they have to pretend to be unabashedly starry-eyed for one another, even after thirty years of bickering and no sex. The only females on earth that actually *enjoy* Valentine's Day are little girls who know that they are getting heart shaped chocolates from Daddy...chicks that happen to start dating a guy in the second week of January, so it is still new and exciting when Feb 14th rolls around... and the few women on the planet that have been lucky enough to marry the guy that will buy them diamonds, no matter how long they have gone without a blow job...

Saint Patrick's Day is the day that people decide that they are Irish, deserve to be kissed for it, and ferociously pinch people on the fat part of the back of their arm for not wearing green. I have to say, as an Irish girl, I *hate* whiskey, I despise Car Bombs, and I find men with moss colored teeth decidedly unattractive. Please, someone tell me how Bennigan's became the hot spot, how on earth beads have anything to do with a kid that was nabbed by Irish Raiders when he was sixteen and enslaved for years only to have to plan his escape and fight for his life to return to his family, or how anyone finds Bailey's Irish Cream as delicious as they make it look in the slo-mo commercials... Sorry, I lost my original train of thought... Oh yeah...drinking nights...Happy Hangover.....

America's Birthday. This is probably the best night of the year as far as I am concerned. Barbeques, fireworks, beer...It really doesn't get any better than that. Flags are flying, candid shots from the Washington Monument are popping into your head, you are jumping in the pool and then wrapping in a warm towel, and being handed a burger. These are the things that make Americans happy. Knowing that no one is going to run up on us screaming in some weird language and pointing a gun at our face for wearing a bikini... listening to the Star Spangled Banner as we leave the cookout and head to work... No more words are necessary to point out how amazing this day is. Although the red, white and blue shooters may merit a mention, they are but an accompaniment to a glorious celebration of Freedom.

Mother's Day. The mother of all holidays. If you work at a restaurant that serves brunch, you are completely screwed. You might as well grab a cot, and set up shop in the walk-in the night before, because you are in for the long haul. Make sure you kissed your mother the Friday before, because you won't see her *ever* again. Setting up, breaking down, cooking even though you are a hostess, popping bottles of champagne even though you are a dishwasher, and getting screamed at for not knowing what side of the plate the fancy fork goes on... It is absolutely crazy, the things that servers and bartenders are subjected to on Mother's Day. Of course, there are flowers for the Mom's, chocolate rivers flowing throughout the dining room, and the world's best sausage gravy there just in case she wants a sample. Even though we all have a mother, it is almost excruciating to endure this kind of chaos. When your shift lasts for *days*, you haven't eaten even though the bacon smells amazing, and you have poured four hundred and forty-four mimosa's in twenty minutes... you begin to curse even your *own* mom, even though she went through painful extremes to expel you safely from her uterus...

Halloween. I get so excited for this night. I suppose it is because I am slightly weird, and thoroughly enjoy the company of other weirdo's. Anything goes on Halloween, although I do chastise the ones who opt for the slutty costumes instead of the spooky spooky. It has become the theme for all hallowed eve as of late, to see what professions we can turn into hookers. Cops, Indians, nurses, army chicks, school girls, mermaids, kittens, mice, etc... its crazy. I always thought we were supposed to scare away the evil spirits, I figure dressing like a whore would only entice them to stay. I personally blame Twilight, (I know, I know, it was turning sexy *way* before that stupid flick) I always associated werewolves with scary, furry, blood thirsty night crawlers... not super ripped Mexican's with pouty lips and sensitive eyes...

Other than ringing in the New Year, Thanksgiving Eve is the most popular night for going out and causing a ruckus. As a complete fan of Turkey Day, I have never gone out drinking the night before, granted I usually have to work, but even if I didn't, I can't imagine that showing up at my mom's house, reeking of vodka and burping up hour old beer, would make me want to eat fourteen deviled eggs, which I have grown rather fond of over the years. I have watched people wash down a few Percocet's with a couple hundred beers, pass out sitting up, drooling like the Mastiff from Turner and Hooch, all before eleven o'clock. My question would be, when they wake up with road rash on their face from sleeping in the parking lot of the bar, how the hell do they explain that to their families upon showing up for the feast?! I guess some people just have a different type of family life. I know that *my* mother would kick my ass, put me on turkey restriction, and assign me to dish duty, while everyone else enjoys a nap and a piece of fresh pumpkin pie...

Christmas parties. Good Lord, why do people even show up? First of all, Fellas, the rented tux is, *without question*, being returned with a vomit stain down the left leg. And Ladies, the gown will undoubtedly end up over your head at one point or another in the evening. Your boss will never get as drunk as you, and the probability of you getting fired or banging the mail clerk in a bathroom stall is greater than the chances of actually strolling in on Monday morning, bright eyed and bushy-tailed, with no incriminating photos of yourself circulating through office emails....

The extremes with which *bar owners* go to these days is almost *outrageous*. The beads, the bands, the champagne glasses, the costumes, the pre-ordering of cases, kegs, and green food coloring. You almost get as stoked as they want you to be, but one thing blasts through your subconscious as quickly as the hatchet falls on the Thanksgiving turkeys' head...SOBRIETY CHECK POINTS...

Of course, the cops *also* know that these are the biggest boozing nights of the year, and while you pretend that the eighteen shots you have done are going to wear off in good time, you find yourself asking if it is okay if you just pass out on the couch in the office... or attempt to drive, knowing full well that you are going to resist the confiscation of your keys, insist that you are fine, and catch a DUI on your way home...all because it is a stupid Holiday. What sucks *the most* is the moment that you **wake up**... curled in a fetal position, on the cold, hard bench in the jail cell that you don't remember walking into, with a headache that has spilt you from asshole to aorta, with no toothbrush, no cell phone, no *pants*, and absolutely no recollection of the reasons behind this curious turn of events. And then, the realization that you haven't even *started* wrapping presents...that's when you sigh and utter the words..."Fuck my *life*..."

Chapter Eighteen
THEN AND NOW

The Evolution of Promiscuity...

In earlier times, when prostitutes doubled as beer wenches, it was basically understood that scoring some action whilst partaking in the nectar of the Gods was pretty much par for the course. Back in those perilous times, tossing a Shilling or two onto the tray of the corset sporting strumpet, was no more passé than strolling casually down to the street corner, kissing a trollop on the hand, and escorting her off to a fifty cent room, while your wife and kids sat in the carriage singing Kumbaya...

Awesomely enough, the tides have shifted, and things don't work like this anymore. It has been an interesting process...over the past hundred years or so, and well, the bartenders have had the front row seat.

Going from The Whore to King Shit has not been an overnight transformation. It has been a tedious, struggling, if not murderous climb up the food chain, and while we admire those before us, we refuse to *ever* again be associated with sleeping with the scum of society. In a strange and incredible turn of events, the minxes have become the untouchable, rather than the buyable. *But*, there are always those ready and willing to offer up conversation, companionship, and a certain level of fraternization. These however, are *not* the bartenders. *Then*, there are The Bar Sluts. The new breed of women that have tossed fifties-style class straight out the window and go right for the booty dropping. No holds barred- these chicks are not only scantily clad, but are bodaciously giving their beer bottles mock blow jobs and insisting that you buy them a shot of Patron. And then another, and maybe four more...just the right amount to render them incapable of saying 'no' when you demand that they flash your friends, grind on a random passerby, and climb willingly into the backseat of some other dude's Mercedes. The best part about being on the other side; is that we get to sit back and observe. Watching the-attention-craving-mini-skirt- wearing-*SuperDrunk* is one of the highlights of our evening. The performance that these chicks put on is nothing but ammunition, and when the day comes that this girl crosses us, we get to unload all of the seedy details, while laughing hysterically at the bad decisions that she made as a result of too much alcohol.

The process of becoming an admirer of the opposite sex comes from many, many hours of being nervous, skittish, confused, and bewildered. This, of course, is when you are entering puberty... and middle school. The metamorphosis of a schoolgirl into a slut is quicker than can be expected. An unconstrained chaser of the affections from those bearing the Y chromosome, the sleazy decent into adult sluthood. Don't you remember having girlfriends that were shy as a lamb, and during the summer months between eighth grade and freshman year, they suddenly grew boobs and became too "fast" for your mother to actually be okay with you hanging out with them? Yeah. Those are the chicks that now spend every Friday night at the club, dancing their way into retardation, and a possible date-rape situation. The worst part about it is that they really *do* bring it on themselves. Seriously, I have gone out dancing with my girlfriends too, but never once in any of those instances, have I ever left without my friends, shooed my girls away because I was 'hooking up', or gotten into a car with a complete stranger after hiking up my skirt and humping his leg, with the entire bar gazing at my goodies as if I were a late night menu special. These are the exceptional qualities of chicks today. Girls don't aspire to meet Romeo anymore, they aspire to create a spectacle of themselves to the point where a guy becomes *so* horny that he wants to shove her in the bathroom...*at the club*... ugh... so gross.

Perfect example; At my bar we host bikini contests' every few months. These women are beautiful, sexy, and confident enough to stroll through a crowd of two-hundred plus. Stage lights that are bright enough to focus on even the most minute of flaws are shining on their thong clad asses, and yet, they remain poised and professional. They go through the motions of an under classed Miss America contest, answering questions and sharing their likes and dislikes, turn on and turn offs, all to the pleasure of a bunch of two-bit drunk fucks that are laughing, talking over the Emcee, and making obscene gestures the *entire* time. Now, of course, the majority of these girls are extremely young (as the more mature women of the millennium have decided that 'If You've Got It, Flaunt It' is **so** last season) and aren't fully aware of the circumstances that they have managed to place themselves in. So, after the contest was over, and the winner departed, the remaining contestants figured that since they lost, they might as well put on a *show*...

Allow me to sketch a disgusting view of your legacy, Dad. The most degrading song you can possibly imagine, thumping its way over the airways, Nine bikini clad girls in a room full of guys, standing on table tops, straddling chairs, and climbing on top of the deejay booth, all simultaneously shaking their tiny butts, clapping their ass cheeks together like the pole dancers at the strip clubs, flinging their hair around like they are Jennifer Beals in *Flashdance*... All while *every single dude in the room* has his camera phone out, filming this ridiculous montage for later viewing, and, uh, let's face it, we all know what he will be *doing* while *viewing*... Yet, none of these red flags are noted by the femme fatale, as they are simply having the time of their lives. Giggling wildly, not so much because they realize how ridiculous they appear, more in lieu of their fathers disappointment. Congratulations...you have failed at raising your daughter.

But let's get back to the ostentatious. These chicks, the ones that aren't yet women and are no longer *girls*, who are offering up the vagina like an Hor'douvre... waiting for the drunk and hungry to reach for a sample... Every time you glance in their direction, they are dumping their purse out onto the bar, screaming about their cell phone, and/or sorting through what they *think* is their wallet, and realizing that they are, in fact, still **broke**. That is when the really freaky shit happens. They will schmooze their way into your conversation, annoy you to the point where you are obligated to by them a drink just to shut them up, and then they pose for the picture that will pop up when you Google the word *Awful*. So sloppy that she has taken off her shoes because she believes the *shoes* are responsible for her not being able to walk, Beastly Bessie stumbles into the bathroom on her final trip of the evening, and notices that she now resembles a homeless hooker instead of the goddess she was upon arrival, drunk to the point where any guy that dares to take her home is potentially facing charges, because she will wake up and not know who the fuck you are or where she met you.

The end of the night comes, much to their dismay, and **there they are**. The extraordinary, incoherent, gelatinous blobs of disappointment. Hanging on whatever or whoever is the closest, she manages to become even more pathetic by glomming onto the last recognizable person in the room. Disturbingly drunk, slipping off of the toilet and tripping over her purse, with breath that could knock a buzzard off of a Port-A-Potty, this chick is the ultimate definition of embarrassment. The most rewarding moment of the night? When you watch her get carried out the door by *That Guy*. Hope she doesn't mind a scorching case of Herpes.

Word to the wise girlie's; stay close to your friends, don't pick up a drink that you have left unattended, avoid the meatheads, don't flash your boobs for beads, and keep your legs closed *at all times*... Because waking up in the hospital- and finding out that you passed out in the bathroom with your pants down, had to be carted out on a stretcher, and barfed on the adorable EMT- will ruin your weekend. Well, that, and the fact that everyone saw your vagina, because they had to pull your underwear up for you.

Chapter Nineteen
THE ALCOHOLICS

...Not So...Um... *Anonymous*...

If Bacardi is part of your workout regimen, then it is quite possible that you are an alcoholic. If you spend more than four hours a day at the bar, if you have a name like Felix, Bart, or Turk, and if you *never* eat...sadly, you *also* might be an alcoholic. If you have the owners phone number on your speed dial, are on a first name basis with the daytime cook, get free pool, have less than twelve teeth or smoke Winston's, you are *definitely* an alcoholic.

The difference between you and the rest of the world is that you live in a grown-up child's reality. Getting a pension, Social Security, or being on Unemployment has somehow mixed reality in with the freedom, and in the process of diluting the subconscious, every- thing else has fallen by the wayside. Things that matter to normal people, no longer bear the pertinence that they once did. Such as; arriving sober to your court date. Say, maybe showing up *without* bloodshot eyes to your daughter's wedding, or being able to get behind the wheel of a car with a *valid* driver's license...

The one thing that ties them to the rest of the world is they have a *schedule* to keep, too. Their daily routine consists of a time frame. (Although that is subject to change, depending on funds, friends, and taxi availability.) They make their rounds, stopping off at all of their favorite pubs according to when their buddies will be out and about as well. They are the ones that are waiting for *your* bar to open, so that they can be at the bar around the corner by three, which is when they meet up with Hank, who is their ride to the *other* bar at five. Most of the time when observing these firewater fanatics, I wonder what my life would be like if I had nothing better to do with my time than show up at the same bars every day, stand outside and smoke cigarettes *by myself,* order twelve bags of takeout bar food, go home *alone* in a cab, and drink Crown Royal in my underwear, while running the risk of burning my house down due to the fact that I passed out cold with a glass in my hand, and I left the broiler on to reheat my twelve bags of bar food. I can't imagine that I would enjoy this process, yet they all seem to be thrilled with the fact that they have Cheeto fingerprint stains on their furniture, an endless supply of Advil, and a ton of paltry peers to share the laughs with. The funny thing is, they all *hate* each other, and make fun of one another's lifestyle behind each other's backs. Then the next day, they are all joking about the fight that almost broke out between three of them, the previous day, at the eleventh bar that they happened to run into each other at. They are like a codependent group of shit slinging primates. Picking ticks off of one another to help, and then fucking the other one's girlfriend just to spite them... and then laughing about it **together**. Ugh. Weird.

The line between Social Drinker and Stool Pigeon is very fine indeed. You can't get away with showing up three hours early for Happy Hour *every day.* Once a month (if not less) is acceptable. But when you are parked outside your local tavern, even before the bartender arrives, then there might be a reason to start scouting out AA meetings in your area. *'To each his own'* is definitely a great philosophy to have when it comes to the way that you lead your life as an individual, but, this rule does not always apply. Especially when you have the dreaded reputation as the Town Drunk, and on more than one occasion, this reputation has landed you in a complicated web of forgotten fiasco's, tied your name into exaggerated stories, or involved *police,* and/or probation. When you are the only witness to a parking lot robbery that took place three hours *after* the bar closed…it doesn't look so great on your part. If you find that you become the **prime suspect** in said investigation, you really have no one to blame but yourself. I mean, what the hell are you *doing* there a hundred and eighty minutes *after* the bar is closed? Do you have any idea how long a hundred and eighty minutes is in *drunk* time? It's like three or four days, at least. The worst part for you is that no one will ever vouch for you. After all, being associated with the drunk guy is almost like being roommates with Jack the Ripper. You never ever know what the drunk guy is capable of, because, hey, he isn't going to remember it tomorrow anyway…So who is to say that he wouldn't club some old lady to death at the convenience store around the corner..?

The Year of the Sot is not one usually favored in the Chinese Zodiac, and those guys apparently know what they are doing over there…I mean, with all of the new age articles on how to Feng Shui your room, house or *life*, obviously their peace of mind and cultural obligations are steadfast, resilient and somewhat difficult to understand. (Both educationally and decoratively…) Speaking of foreign shit…have you ever listened to a drunk man attempt to order a drink or have a conversation? Please tell me where to locate the subtitles, because I have no fucking idea what you are saying…

To us, the Bartenders, these guys are, for the most part, pretty respectful. They have learned over the years that being thrown out of the bar at two in the afternoon isn't fun, especially when all of their other alcoholic friends are still perched on the stools of seventh heaven, and they find themselves bumbling around outside, sifting through the sands of the flower-pot-turned-ashtray looking for a smoke-able butt, praying that a fellow boozer stumbles out the door in time to save them from their nicotine fit. Most of the time, they are just sad to look at. Even when they are being funny, somewhere in the back of your mind, you feel a tiny twinge of guilt, knowing that you are one of the people contributing to the slow but sure shut down of their mind, body, and soul…But, on the other hand, five bucks is five bucks right? On a good day, when all of the local lushes show up, you are looking at fifty or sixty extra bucks in tips, and let's face it, it's not Show-friends, it's Show-business. If their family members don't care enough to snatch them up by the collar and throw their alcoholic asses in rehab, what the hell am I going to do for them?

Chapter Twenty
COUGAR VS KITTEN

The Clash of the Vagina's...

The Cougars. The Kittens. The very act of being either one of these women is hard for the rest of us. Yet, there they are, waiting, wanting, prowling, dancing, coughing, sweating...*lurking*...standing by for the ambush alert, preparing for that moment that you slip up...and in an incoherent That Guy or Creeper moment take them home...

They are a tad different than the already discussed sluts, but it isn't an ocean that separates them...maybe a creek, or a large puddle... These girls are the ones who go out dressed to impress, whereas the whores are simply dressed like, well, *whores*. Cougars are usually accompanied by other cougars, just like the actual animal, they travel in packs. Kittens are smaller, cuter, and have sometimes been abandoned in a garden shed, waiting for someone with a big heart to come along and adopt them.

Cougars usually have more of an attitude, as they have noticed from the moment that they entered the bar, that us, the bartenders, are getting way more attention on accident then they can hope to get on purpose, *all night*. It's not our fault, again, there is just something attractive to the men, about a drink slinging, sports loving lady, who isn't sitting at the bar waiting for someone to notice her. Depending on the bar, the cougars are a bit wealthier than the rest of the patrons, and while the sluts might hop in your lap at the mention of a taking a shot, *these* weathered ladies... **they hold out**, waiting for the perfectly stupid frat boy to stumble into her web and sigh with dreamy desire as the 'older woman' fantasy plays out in explicit detail in his minds' eye. Catching these cats early, and smiling even though it is forced, making them awesome martini's, and laughing with them is usually the way to nix any attitude in the bud, avoiding the claws to the mid section. Once the Cougars are on your side, smooth sailing from that point on, they will tip heavy, and attract the men, who will also tip heavy, and therefore everybody wins. They get their much needed attention, you get to pay your car insurance, *and* go shopping the next day, and the smiles are endless. Same goes for the Kitten. If you catch them when they first walk in, they will think you are the bee's knees, screaming your name and telling everyone in the room that she loves you, you are the coolest, most 'bestest' bartender that has ever lived. Even though the tips aren't exactly stellar, you have gained yourself a new regular, and she will bring all of her little kitty friends in to admire you and ramble on about how awesome you are. While it becomes irritating occasionally, *everyone* likes a fan club. It's another one of the perks.

Now that we have gone through the background details of these frisky felines, we can skip ahead to the fun stuff. Have you ever been to a bar and had a group of old chicks fighting a group of young chicks for the attention of the only twelve guys in the room? No? Well, let me assure you- it is fucking *hilarious*. When the old chicks pull out the money, buying shots and beers in effort to try and persuade the men to focus their gallantry on her newly bought breasts, the young chicks simply parade around the bar, with their perky boobies and flat stomachs, in their low rise jeans and Ugg boots, completely confusing the men, and pissing off the old chicks. See how the yoyo goes up and down? It is hard for the Cougars, and sometimes I feel bad for them. Knowing that one day, I will be an older woman, and while it is cool to think that by *that* time, some young, hot college kid will still have fantasies about seeing me naked, I can pretty much guarantee that I will never be desperate enough to go out with my *other* old ass girlfriends and try to take one of them home. Face it ladies, the bar is full of young, dumb, *opportunities* for the guys. No way are they spending an evening strolling on a beach with you, listening to you babble about your divorce, when they *could* be in a hot tub with the kittens, possibly having the best one night stand of their measly little existences. My advice to the woman over thirty five? If you want to go to the bar to have fun, by all means, **go**. If you want to meet a man, try EHarmony

Chapter Twenty One
EQUAL OPPORTUNITY EMPLOYER

*"I Don't Discriminate...I Hate **Everyone**..."*

When the Bi-Weekly 'mandatory' meeting rolls around, and everyone is gathered in the bar, at fucking nine in the morning on a Sunday, still wearing pajamas, smoking and drinking coffee like it is their *job...* The owner likes to have a portion of this meeting designated for new ideas. Usually, this brings on a barrage of stupid suggestions conjured up by waitresses, (who don't really know what the hell they are talking about anyway) that all get shot down by one bartender or another. My idea is always the same. A two sided bar. One side for normal people, and one with an express lane for idiots. For some reason, my boss never jumps on this concept. **I,** and I don't think that I'm alone here, think that it is a brilliant scheme. Planning who would be scheduled to pour for the retards, however, is where the plan always falls apart. No one wants to volunteer to have their night shit on by a bunch of poo throwing baboons. Which brings me to elaborate on the reasons why I really *do* hate *everyone.*

Over the years I have come to the realization that most people are completely lacking common sense. If God picked a group of people that would automatically be granted entrance to Heaven, it would undoubtedly be the Bartenders of the world. Why? Because the rest of humanity has no idea what it is like. Example number one. Have any of you ever cleaned the bathroom at your office and

86

found a pregnancy test bobbing in the toilet? No? How about a Douche bottle in the sink? Maybe shit-covered panty hose in the tampon disposal box? Yeah. That's what waits for us at the end of the night in the Ladies' room. Instead of 'Ladies' room, I have often thought we should hang a sign that says 'Disgusting Fucks', but then I think girls might be confused about where to go and douche, while at the club...Seriously, if you are having a not-so-fresh moment, I think you'd better just call it a night. And if you need to know if you are pregnant *that* bad...**go the fuck home**.

How about if in a rare *nice* moment...you are actually attempting to help a slovenly hobgoblin to their car and they puke on you. Or while walking back from the kitchen with four plates of food balancing on your arms, you unknowingly pass through a fight, and get knocked out by a flying barstool. That is *always* fun. What if you are an innocent bystander to a domestic dispute, and get shot in the face...? These are the dangers that people in ordinary jobs never once encounter, or even *think* about when punching the time clock. They are also the reasons that we are the only ones allowed to utter that phrase. I hate everyone. Because people suck. *All* people.

People that don't tip. People that play Keno. People with polluted attitudes. People that go to the bar with no money and bum drinks off of the other People. People that smell. People that always want a hug, even though you just met them. People that show up at noon, when you haven't even set the bar up yet. People that bring their mentally disabled mothers to the bar and make them sit there all day, while they proceed to get shitfaced with their friends. People that argue. People that never say a word. People that preach. People that cheat, and expect you to lie for them if their wife calls. People that stay too long. People that don't tip. People that play Keno. People that don't remember your name, when you have been pouring their beers for a year and a half. People that call you boo boo or mommy. People that cry at the bar. People that do coke in the bathroom and think that you can't figure out why their eyes are as big as dinner plates. People that complain. People that call you a bar maid. People that blow their nose while sitting at the bar, then put the tissue *on the bar*. People that eat chicken wings. People that don't tip. People that play Keno. People that leer. People that get mad when they have just arrived, and someone else is sitting in 'their' seat. People that *call* it 'their' seat. People that drool. People that insist on showing you pictures of their friend-that-you-have-never-mets'- wedding. People that bring their kids to the bar. People that wear leather jackets in the summer. People that tell you what goes in a drink. People that chew with their mouths open. People that gulp loud enough for me to hear. People that ask what the specials are. People that don't tip. People that play Keno.

These are just some of the people that I hate. Of all of those mentioned, there are a few that I need to describe for the readers in more detail. The guy/girl with no money. This piece 'o shit is the most notorious of all nuisances. As soon as he hits the front door, people sigh and turn their backs, hoping to go unnoticed by the penniless podge, *or* they jam their wallet into their pocket and ask for the check. Setting off a chain reaction for people bailing out early, therefore pissing off the barkeep as well. And then on top of it, when he orders a drink from the bartender, he will do everything in his power to avoid paying for it. **Forever**. Then the girl version of this jackass is sometimes even *worse*. If the boss is somewhat of a sucker for a pretty face, this bitch will order drinks on his tab all night long. Smiling at the bartender like we are supposed to know who she is, she then gets and attitude after you tell her how much it costs. "Well, I'm on (insert bosses name here)'s tab." Oh really? I thought he was only buying you ONE, you fucking mooch. Seriously… who the hell goes out with no money? **Our** local bar-broke-regular was bellied up the other day, ordered a two dollar draft, nursed it for an hour, then told me (as he was handing me two dollars *exactly*) that he was going to need the rest of his money to pay the cover charge that they were going to charge him to stay in the bar after 9pm. My thoughts? First of all, if you left the house with seven dollars in your pocket and expected to make it through and entire Saturday night, you are a donkey, and secondly, how are you going to drink anymore after that cover charge gets paid? Well, he did what he *always* does; he bummed enough drinks to keep him happy for the rest of the night. Meanwhile, I was behind the bar praying for one of the Grab-oids from *Tremors* to shoot up out of the floor and suck him down into the earth, screaming for someone to save him. No hysteria here, I would have dropped a dollar into the things mouth and pat it on the head, grinning merrily as I watched it drag that fucker away.

Hey you- yeah *you*- **Huggy**, you're next. Why do you think you can hug me? Why would you ask for a hug? I don't even know you dude. So step off with that shit. Let's be honest here. No girl is ever *unaware* that you are just trying to feel her boobs against you, and it comes off as weird and creepy, so knock it off, or I will pee in your Coors Lite.

For those that can't find a babysitter, please, for the love of God, stay **home**. You are the worst parents alive. Your kids do not belong here. This is not the Kiddie Academy. It is a bar. People are cussing, drinking, fighting, puking, trying to play pool, or watch football, and your little ankle biters are making it difficult for us to enjoy it. I don't want to have to watch my mouth. If I wanted to do that, *I* would have stayed home. Taking your kid to the local pub, handing them eight bucks for video games and throwing crackers at them does not constitute spending quality time with Junior on a Sunday night. Doesn't that snot nose have school tomorrow? Oh, and just so you know... *everyone* in the bar is talking shit about you. Take your kid home.

You 'specials' bastards. I hate to point out the obvious, but, when you walk in and say "What are the specials?" you are sending a very clear, undisputable message. I AM CHEAP. I almost want to hand you a Twix and tell you to think it over before making the bartenders think that you spend your afternoons looking for excellent deals on Ban Lon smocks at Bargain Mart. A tip to help you avoid embarrassing moments; If you are in fact, a cheap asshole that can't afford to go out without a budget, scout out the 'specials' boards that are literally *everywhere* in the bar, and then casually order the draft that happens to be two bucks, as if you were going to order it anyway. We have no idea that you aren't a Natural Light drinker when you sit down, unless you ask what the cheapest beer is, and *then* ask for a Natural Light. Get it? Or, you can just do what every bartender on the planet would prefer... go get a case of *PBR* for eight dollars and stay the hell home.

Ok. Now for *you*. Stop calling me babygirl. Or mommy. I am not a baby and I am definitely not your mom. Is it hard to say Bartender? Here, try it with me. "***Bar-ten-der***." What is with the boo boo shit? Do you see Yogi standing nearby? Is there a picnic basket looped over my arm? No? Then stop calling me that.

And finally...People that play Keno. Let me explain something to you, friend. Your Keno slip is the most annoying thing I have ever seen in my whole **life**. I mean that. In no way is that piece of paper as important to me as it is to you. Therefore, shoving it in my face, bitching about not getting your ticket run in time for the next game, waving money at me or calling me names is not going to get me to walk toward that ridonculous pink machine any faster. You know what might work? TIPPING. For those of you that act like it is imperative that I get your ticket in, and then I see that you just had me running down the bar for a damn *dollar* ticket... I hate you the most. Really, you can't win anything by playing a one dollar ten spot with no bonus. The most incredible Keno story I have hails from about six years ago. A man who was not a regular but wasn't a complete stranger was sitting at the bar with a stack of about fifty Keno cards. The eew factor about this, is that they were already filled out when he walked in. He had them stored in a long, flat, wrinkle deflecting plastic sleeve, with a little matching pencil. So I knew he meant business. The problem with running fifty Keno cards at one time is that sometimes, Keno has a mind of its own and you might have to run the same ticket two or three times in order for the stupid machine to take it. Which means that sometimes, all fifty tickets might not get run in the two-minute-and-sixteen-second interval that runs between games. Anyway, this guy got pissed at me on the third or fourth time that I ran his fifty card set. Whatever. He was drinking Jack Daniels by the pint glass, at four o'clock in the afternoon so his feelings toward me weren't really going to make me lose any sleep. So, I set out making about twelve shots for the service bar and as I was pouring, he decided it was time to play another round. "Run these again for me, would ya?" He asked, holding out the Keno cards. Mind you, I have a tumbler in one hand and I am lining up shot glasses with the other so I just looked at him and said, "Sure, give me a minute." He grunted in disappointment. "In a minute, I will miss the game." He said angrily. So I set a glass down, and with my free hand I pointed at the sign above the bar that read **Drinks Before Keno**. Without saying a word, I went back to my task. This is where he blew it. He tossed the Keno cards at me, called me the C word and stormed off to the bathroom. (Where I later found out he had been doing blow all afternoon, which is probably the reason for the impatience and nasty disposition) So I took the shots to service, and went to the office to get the owner. (Which I had also been dating for oh, I don't know, three years or so...) So, my boyfriend/owner comes out and tells him that he has to leave. The guy of course freaks out, almost fights the owner, and finally pays his tab and leaves. Well, there was about two-hundred keno tickets sitting in a pile on the bar that he neglected to take with him, plus his little keno diary, and a slew of pre-filled-out keno cards that were strewn about from him flinging them at my face. So I gathered up the tickets, sauntered over to the pink beast, and began checking them. I had gone almost all the way through, only hitting about thirty bucks collectively, until I came across the big one. Most places have a standard amount that they are allowed to pay out on a Keno ticket. Ours was nine hundred dollars. So when I slipped this beauty into the slot and the screen read "Prize too large, retailer not permitted to pay" I got somewhat elated. Unfortunately at the time, Keno wasn't as fancy as it is now, so I had no way of knowing what the prize amount was. So I slipped the ticket in my pocket, didn't say a word, even to my owner/boyfriend, and waited for my relief. **That was the longest shift of my life**. Finally, when I got off, I headed straight for the liquor store. I handed the ticket over, and was handed a set of papers in return. Hmmm, curious. They were tax forms. Apparently my jackpot was *so* big, I was going to have to claim it, and prove that I had no liens against me for child support or HOA's. Sweet! So I filled out the paperwork and when that little china man handed me thirty-five hundred bucks, I nearly jumped across the counter and kissed him. I called my roommates immediately, and we set out for Best Buy. That beautiful HD flat screen TV that I bought? Yeah I still have it. I am actually watching Cheers on it right now. I Bought a new surround sound system too. Priceless. **Instant Karma**. That's what you get for calling me a cunt. I waited for a long time to see that guy again. Never happened. I really wanted to tell him about the awesome tip that he left me for my troubles. Maybe it's better that I didn't see him again, I get to live with the satisfaction, and he is probably sitting at a bar somewhere, doing coke and drinking Jack, trying to forget that tiny fortune that he left on a slab of granite, all those years ago...

Remember, what you do in this life echoes into the next. So if you are the disrespectful **asshole** that becomes the reason that people like *me* hate everyone...one day, someone is going to shove a Keno machine straight up your pee hole, your kids are going to turn out **just** like you, the only hug you are going to get is from your cell mate as he sodomizes you, (while calling you boo boo) and you are going to be bumming drinks off of **Hitler**... in Hell.

Oh, and for the record, if you call it Lager, instead of *Yuengling* when you are ordering it, I want you to die. And, keep your God Damned fingers out of my fruit tray, this isn't a buffet...

Chapter Twenty Two
DEAR ALCOHOL...

First and foremost, let me tell you that I am a huge fan of yours. My dear friend, you can always be counted upon when truly needed. A post work cocktail, a friendly beer with the pals at the pub, you are even around during the holidays, hidden inside of chocolates and swirling through the punch bowl, comforting me when I am smack dab in the middle of a family gathering that has taken a turn for the worse. (As Uncle Joe has decided that even though he is fifty pounds too large, he is going to be the one that dons the Santa Suit, and unfortunately becomes lodged in the chimney, causing the children to become hysterical...)

Lately though, I have begun to question your intentions. While I want to believe that you have my best interests at heart, I feel that your influence has led to a few somewhat 'questionable' decisions, resulting in devastating consequences. Example; DRUNK DIALING. While I agree that communication is important, I question the suggestion that any conversation of substance or necessity takes place after 2 am. In what way is encouraging me to call my ex-boyfriends, ex best-friends, mother-in-law, or truly despised nemesis's, benefiting our relationship? It really only brings about fitful dreams, nausea, and a post phone call sense of stupidity, that is then magnified upon waking up, *sober*, and realizing that I have made a complete fool out of myself. You aren't helping my ego, Alcohol. Isn't that your *JOB*?

And what of the eating? My diet is wrecked because of you. For some ungodly reason, you have **made** me decide that cooking beefaroni, ordering a pizza, baking potatoes au gratin, snacking on vanilla ice cream and green olives, concocting a strange tuna salad sandwich, attempting to flip an omelet- that inevitably becomes stuck to the ceiling- and washing it all down with the left over Natty Bo, is not *only* a good idea, but an absolute essentiality. Doritos topped with queso, and chili as a side dish? I think you went too far this time... I don't even *eat* chili....

The clumsiness. Ahh, the clumsiness...If you are insinuating that I need to participate in Yoga classes to improve my balance, it's cool, but there are other ways to bring about the topic of conversation... there is no need to force me to fall over into a pile of my own vomit.. or someone *else's* for that matter, just to hammer the point home. I get it. Waking up with bruises, which are gigantic and gross in color, is also unnecessary, for you have imbedded the vitality of sobriety by causing me to fall out of my car, and scrape my face *and* my new tattoo across the pavement... And for the record, *before* putting me through this treacherous ordeal, it should not take more than forty-five seconds to get my key into the lock... **Dick**...Quit fucking with my head....

Furthermore, the hangovers have *got* to stop. I am aware that a certain amount of penance for my previous night of debauchery is in order, but this is getting ridiculous. When four o'clock in the afternoon arrives, and I am still incapable of peeling the contact lenses out of my eyes, or dragging myself out of bed, even though my dog is pawing at my face, then sitting by the door, whining because she hasn't pee'd in twelve hours... I blame YOU, friend. My entire day is **shot**. (Ugh...don't say *shot*...) I ask that, if the proper precautions are taken (water, vitamin B, bread products, aspirin) prior to going to sleep, or passing out face down on the kitchen floor with a bag of popcorn, the hangover should be minimal and in no way interfere with my daily activities...

Alcohol...I have enjoyed our friendship for many years now and I would like to ensure that we remain on good terms. You have been the invoker of excellent stories, the provocation for countless hours of laughter, and the much needed companion when I just don't know *what* to do with the extra money in my pockets. In order to continue this friendship, I ask that you carefully review my grievances and get back to me no later than Thursday (ladies night) by three o'clock (pre happy-hour) on your possible solutions. Hopefully we can continue this fruitful partnership, for I would be downright distraught if we were to break up... going cold turkey at this point is just not in the cards for me. I will never say that I **cannot** live without you, I *can* live without you...I just don't want to...

P.S. There are a few things you should know that I put up with from you, even after we have parted ways for the night.

THINGS THAT ARE DIFFICULT TO SAY WHEN DRUNK.
1. Innovative. 2. Preliminary. 3. Proliferation. 4. Cinnamon

THINGS THAT ARE *VERY* DIFFICULT TO SAY WHEN DRUNK.
1. Specificity. 2. British Constitution. 3. Passive-aggressive disorder. 4. Phonetically.

THINGS THAT ARE DOWNRIGHT *IMPOSSIBLE* TO SAY WHEN DRUNK.
1. Thanks, but I don't want to have sex. 2. Nope, no more beer for me. 3. Sorry, but you're not really my type. 4. Good evening officer... isn't it lovely out tonight...?

Chapter Twenty Three
THE EX FILES

*"I **hate** that he saw me naked..."*

When working at a bar, you occasionally run into those that used to share a few sexually decorated moments in your past. For some, those periods of time are impossible to recover from. *The one that got away...* in more modern terms and to those that don't appreciate *passion*, this can be loosely translated as 'that guy who fucked me over and broke my heart.' *This* guy walking into your already abrasive atmosphere can be super distracting, and where you do your best to pretend that he doesn't exist, you find yourself heading towards the Corona cooler or the Tuaca machine, just because he is sitting next to it, and for an unearthly reason unbeknownst to you, he **has** to see how *fantastic* you look that night. Eat your heart out...fucker.

On the other hand, the straggler walks in, and when he becomes obsessed with the fact that he used to date you, shouting it out while drunkenly reaching for his shot of Jameson, doing the annoying arm tap thing that so many of them do, you find yourself snarling and turning away, with the 'nose-vomit-slash- I-really-need-a-fucking-shot' face that only an I-appreciate-the-ex-factor-coworker truly understands, she/he casually leads you away, pouring you a super cold, extra large, value meal sized shot of vodka, attempting to console you, while you toss it back, wiping the eew drizzle from your chin, smugly hating the fact that you were ever stupid enough to take that guy seriously... even if it was solely for the sex.

In an almost conspirator manner, the exes seem to figure out when you are *finally* over them...and then they *find* you... Showing up and smiling knowingly...asking if you want to make out...when they already know that the answer is *duh*! (Meet me in the alley in five minutes...) It's like they have nothing better to do than make your life miserable. But, damn, what a great kisser...

I almost got married once. I had the dress and everything. About three weeks before the wedding I called it off and years went by without me seeing or thinking about this idiot. Wouldn't you know it? He walked into my bar a few weeks ago, with his new girlfriend. Now, if he would have sat at a table or at the other end of the bar, I might have been able to ignore the fact that he was there. But no, no. That would make things too easy. Of course, as soon as he spotted me, he called out my name, and then had me running for his drinks for the rest of the night. The reason for me not refusing service and telling him to fuck off? He is a bartender too. And I knew that the tip would be well worth my pride swallowing troubles. And it was. Aside from the fact that I had to listen to him tell everyone of my regulars, co-workers and even the strangers that I was his ex-fiancée, and ignoring how much I was tasting bile in the back of my throat, it wasn't as unpleasant as I thought it would be. Guess he grew up slightly. Still, I felt bad for his girlfriend. She was the one that had to sit there while he bragged to everyone around him about the fact that I almost married him. Can't say that I'm sorry about the decision I made...

Ex boyfriends that are still in love with you are the worst. The sad little puppy dog faces. The over tipping. The awful attempts to drag you down Memory Lane. Seriously, if you show up at my bar, all I am going to do is hurt your feelings, so it's probably wise for you to stay away if you know that I work there. We broke up for a reason buddy. It's not Memory Lane to me, it's Dirt Street.

The ones that you *forgot* you dated are kind of funny. Like the random guy that shows up and says…"Hey…didn't we go out in middle school?" Wow man. Middle school is a cloudy haze in my brain that has been replaced with more recent and less embarrassing memories. And no, we didn't 'go out'- technically, because I was *twelve* and my parents didn't let me *go* anywhere. So, just because we passed notes in the halls, doesn't mean we dated. Unless you look like Johnny Depp. Then the answer is *yes*. We dated for a long, long time.

Chapter Twenty Four
THE CRAZIES

Every town has a few loony toons. You know, the guy that you see jogging backwards down the highway, the old lady that stands around in her front yard holding a machete... There is nothing wrong with pointing these people out. They just have a few screws loose. The only thing to worry about with these folks, is, they don't *know* that they have a few screws loose. So when one of them walks into the bar, you want to stand outside holding a sign with a blinking arrow, and charge admission for the show that is about to take place inside. I have had quite a few run-ins with the crazies since my debut, and it seems like the more years that pass, the crazier the fucking crazies get!

A lady named Mary would come into the bar, sit quietly and order a glass of Chardonnay. Of course she was only quiet for about ten minutes, and then her meds would wear off. She would talk to the empty stool next to her, and ask if it wanted to split a crab dip with her. Very bizarre. One day she walked in with a dog, and I told her that she could not bring the hound inside. She asked who she was supposed to chat with, if the dog wasn't allowed to sit with her. I told her to talk the stool like she did every other day. She got really mad at me and drove her car through the front window of the building.

An old-as-Moses guy named Al used to wander around our parking lot, picking up trash, and hunting for butts. Occasionally he would come inside and ask for water or coffee. One day he decided to change his incontinence pad in our bathroom, but he forgot to throw his old one in the trash, or put on a new one for that matter... and then he shit in his pants. Well, mostly in his pants. Some of it was also on the toilet seat, and on the floor. My boss was thoroughly pissed when he had to spend the remainder of his afternoon, scrubbing poo off of the linoleum, and trying to get the door guys to stop playing 'kick the diaper'.

There was a chick named Margaret that would come in, and cry. Every day. She wasn't really 'crazy', just an attention seeking hypochondriac. But it wasn't like the normal hypochondriac stuff like strep throat or bunions. She had always *just* been diagnosed with some sort of terminal illness. Tuesday she had cervical cancer, but Wednesday she had a tumor detected in her brain stem. She was always better the moment someone bought her a drink and suddenly her bunions or cervix weren't preventing her from doing the running man across the dance floor. What an ass.

The crazies are all around us. Many levels of crazy. There is a guy named Kelvin that comes in every day and just talks. Talks, talks, talks. He's the guy that will walk up to you and say "hey, what's that you are eating?" (Just to start a conversation so he can talk, talk, talk.) When you roll your eyes and look at him blankly and say "Uh...*French fries.*" With a drop dead tone, and a 'you fucking moron, you know they are French fries' look, he changes the subject and then laughs loudly at his own stupid joke, like it is the funniest damn thing he has ever heard. The 'on demand fart' would come in handy right now, but you have to save them all for the creepers that will be surrounding your car in the parking lot. This guy can never take a hint, and he continues to talk, even when you are standing there with your back turned on him, doing a cross word, watching TV, or talking on the phone. You sigh when you see him hit the front door, because you know no matter how hard you try to ignore him, you will be hearing his stupid voice in your sleep, as he laughs his way into your nightmare.

Some people are only crazy when they are sober. Some of them are only crazy when they are drunk. Some of them are only crazy before they get their morning coffee. Oh, wait…that's **me**. Some of them obsess crazily about things that only make sense to other crazy people. There are ones who wander around talking to themselves about the impending doom of 2012, then other ones who swear that a terrorist is going to walk in the bar at any minute and blow us all to smithereens. A few days a week we are subjected to other peoples craziness, and yet we are somehow expected to remain sane and professional. I have let my crazy flag fly a few times when dealing with the ultra-crazy **swingers** that used to gather every Thursday afternoon for happy hour. Warding off swinger advances is different than any other experience known to man. These people really are certifiable. They live in their own little world, where it is not at all strange to offer to trade spouses, with twelve other people, and hey, let's toss in a terrified bartender to make the evening a little more exciting. Seriously, until I figured out that they were swingers, I thought that they were just *weird people*. The moment it dawned on me that they were like the Free Masons, only with more nudity and not as *secret* of a society, I started texting friends to come up and sit at the bar, so I would have some normal people to talk to. Because any indication of even remotely *attempting* at a casual conversation with one of these bedlamites, went from nothing to ninety in about three seconds flat. Suddenly, you are invited to spend a weekend in their hot tub, and being offered a hand massage. I'd hate to see this group on ecstasy…

No matter where you are, or what you do, you will run into a crazy at one point or another in your life. But, *you* lucky bastards never have to hang out with them for more time than it takes to say, "Whoa, that dude is fucking nuts!" and walk away. Unfortunately, **we** have to *hope* that at the end of the crazy train, there is a tip in the caboose. If not, it just seems unfair that we have to watch the crackpot channel all afternoon.

Chapter Twenty Five
ORGANIZED CHAOS

A Method to the Madness

Ever tried to correlate a riot? Manage the melee? Well that's what working in a busy bar is like, on a daily basis, for all of us. Running around like a chicken with its head cut off, shouting for back up bottles of Patron or Hennessey, squeezing past other bustling bartenders, keeping up with the service printer that just won't stop fucking ticking, running food, trying to figure out why there is no clean glass, and *fuming* because the ice bins are empty. When an establishment houses forty employees that are all hauling ass, the POS system totally crashes, the power goes out, the two retarded managers are too busy scouting out chicks to get you change, and the bar back keeps running to the bathroom because he decided that eating shrimp casserole on a Saturday afternoon the *day* before the Super Bowl would be a good idea, things can get a tad out of control. This is when we are supposed to rally together and make it through the night as a unified group. That whole 'there is no *I* in team' thing rarely upholds, and people resort to a more primitive way of thinking...i.e., there *is* an *I* in "You fucking Idiots! Get it together!" But of course, no one is listening. This results in more mayhem, and then the world as we know it slowly begins to unravel. Most of the time, the breakdown happens in groups. At first everyone is *actually trying* to help each other. Steering their comrades through the dark, helping them handwrite the tabs that they can actually *remember*, until the BG&E guys show up to fix the power outage. (Never mind the obvious thing to do, which would be to *close* because no one can *see*, closing is not an option. The owner will laugh right in your face for even bringing it up.) The bartenders remain true to each other and one of them assigns themselves to service bar, taking call out orders from the waitresses. The managers are outside on the phone, for hours it seems, calling up to the heavens and praying that the electric bill got paid, and the door guys are doing their very best to have *every one's* back. Over the course of a few hours, one, two, three things begin to happen, that shift the tides and cause the breaking of Pangaea. Dividing gradually into smaller formations, coworkers begin to forego the earlier ideals of unity, and lean more towards pack mentality. Each pack silently elects an Alpha, and the others fall into place. This works for a few *more* hours, and then, after rigorous mental tortures have made their bodies tell their minds that it is every man for himself, the troops begin to disassemble altogether. The resulting casualties can only be blamed upon the owner, who refused to take into consideration that a battle fought by the blind *cannot* be won.

When nights like this happen, friendships are put to the test, work ethics are thoroughly called into order, and Darwinism becomes *law*. Only the strong survive. At the end of this assessment of one's loyalty, when the power company has finally restored the sun to our tiny universe, we then send out the search party. We locate those that have muscled through, figure out who has slipped out the back door, save the one that is hiding in the walk in, and finally stumble upon the *noble* one, who is surveying the damage with honor, and perhaps scribbling the Bar Spangled Banner down on a bev-nap, in a teary eyed moment of triumph.

When dealing with a crowded room of strangers, who are all on a mission to melt away their own worries with alcohol, having people with 'problems' as the ones who are serving it is not always a great idea. This is why a standard rule of thumb applies for all persons who engage in serving the public. Leave your shit at the door. It doesn't matter to the thirsty turtles snapping for a drink if your dog died, if you just found out that you are knocked up, or if your husband emptied out your bank account to run off with his dental hygienist. Bringing your baggage *into* the bar, only adds more drama to the night for the rest of us, and when we are spending more time asking *you* if *you* are ok, than serving the *customers*, it causes a systematic disintegration of regulation, leaving our world open to destruction. Angry mobs of jerks, reaching over the bar, pushing, shoving, fighting, complaining… and we have gotten so far behind that we just can't catch up. *Then*, a manager who has never bartended before attempts to come behind the bar to 'help', and the ensuing crumble of our night, that was previously only *teetering* on collapse, then becomes inevitable. They are ringing up drinks on the wrong tab, getting in the way, pissing everybody off, and wasting more booze than he or she is selling. I have actually stopped, looked around, and thought that I saw Bruce Willis in a space suit coming to my rescue, just as the asteroid was ready to smack me in the face… After snapping out of that glorious illusion, and back to reality…I *then* stopped, looked around, and prayed for the fucking asteroid.

Chapter Twenty Six
THE SOUVENIRS

A Tale of Too Much Booze

So….On my thirtieth Birthday I climbed out of a limo, that was literally the size of my apartment…stood by as my girlfriend shoved me out of the way, and totally bogarted the only toilet at the gas station. *She* then watched, as I made the scarring decision to pee in the sink, and laughed maniacally as the sink fell off of the wall, with me in it, and crashed to the floor. After I hit the ground, with my pants around my knees and broken chunks of porcelain and metal surrounding me, her laughter slowly turned into a scream, and she began frantically pointing at my arm, while hovering above the toilet. No *way* that just happened… Unfortunately, it did. I wish that it hadn't, but, I make bad choices.

"Dude, I think I'm fucked up." I said, as I studied the gaping holes in my flesh. Strangely, they were the only words I could summon, but then again, I still really had to pee. After she wrapped my arm in an entire roll of paper towels, we began planning our escape route. We still had a blood caked key that needed to be returned to the cashier, and it looked like I hit that sink with a fucking sledge hammer, so we knew the police would inevitably be involved. It was my birthday, so naturally, the smorgasbord of alcohol and, um, other means of intoxication that were stashed in the limo would no doubt earn us a few days in the pokey. So we opted for the quick departure. Tossing the key to the attendant as we passed, hoping he wouldn't notice the blood soaking through the paper towel and running down my arm, we hauled ass to the limo. One thing that this experience taught me was that, while '*when you gotta go, you gotta go*' is a very, *very* true statement, sometimes just waiting the five extra seconds for the toilet is a lot more practical for the well being of your appendages.

Four magical words that have preceded almost every injury that either myself or my friends have sustained over the years? *Dude, hold my beer*...

This chapter is dedicated to the scars, bruises, mental anguish and *Oh Shit* moments that are always accompaniments to long, hard nights of drinking. Like that time I was in Mexico, and had way too many margarita's to actually *listen* to the instructor, that was trying to explain to us *exactly* how to jump off of that **cliff**, into the fresh water well, *I* barreled past everyone, woo-hooing as I jumped…and broke my ankle. Everyone has a story. I, myself, have over a dozen, at **least**. *But*, I also get to partake in observing the idiots, which means I don't feel like *too* much of a jackass when I go drunk snowboarding and eat shit so hard that it jars my teeth loose. I suppose that I am just guilty of overzealous ideas about my own mortality, as a result of over*consumption* of alcohol.

Ever wake up with a black eye and find it extremely difficult to remember why or when someone's fist landed on your face? Ever find yourself with unidentifiable scrapes along your knees and elbows? What of the humiliating scrapes that aren't actually *scrapes*, but turn out to be rug burn..? Ever seen a piece of an elevator come flying out of a tailgate *directly* at someone's head, as they go skidding across an icy blacktop? How is it possible to wake up in a different condition than you *thought* you were in when you went to sleep? Piecing together the puzzle explaining your newfound physique is not something you want to be doing with a wicked hangover, *especially* after finding your pinky toe on the floor in the kitchen, next to a box of Milk Bones... considering the fact that you don't even have a *dog*...

What is the culprit behind these mysterious injuries? What kind of miscreant would knowingly induce this kind of confusion? Who on Earth would volunteer to be the guilty party responsible for the hundreds of dollars worth of hospital bills and the physical therapy required to recover from said impairments? I'll bet you five dollars that his name is one of the following. Jack. Jim. Johnny. Jameson. Jose. Granddad. And if it isn't one of *these* suspects, it is a minion from Hell, sent to teach you a lesson from the Smirnoff family's Book of Counted Sorrows. There. Now you owe me your lunch money.

I have watched people jump into fires, throw themselves off of bridges, play catch with lawn darts, flip off of porches, and tie just about *anything* that they can think of to the back of a pick-up truck. I love the fact that, at the time, these things have all seemed like a really good idea. Until, of course, the hospital bill arrives. Do you know how much an ambulance ride costs? If you *don't* know, it just means you need to get out and drink more. There was a guy that started shit with a pool playing regular, egged him on *so* much, that the pool player grabbed a pool ball and launched it at the guys' mouth. I have never seen so much blood before in my life. The moral of the story? If you are looking to find a dentist for a roommate... **this** is the way to go about it. That guy's mouth was fucked up for *months*, and every time I saw him after that, he was fixing his face... one tooth at a time. Oh, and he stayed away from the pool tables.

A friend of mine and I were having lunch (and beer, lots and lots of beer) at a crab house one day, when he suddenly hopped up from the table, pointed at the bridge behind the patio (which was filled with lots of other people having beer and crabs) and said "I'm going to go jump off of that bridge," and walked away. I sat there, trying to figure out this curious turn of events, when I saw him hiking up the shoulder of the overpass, trying not to get hit by a bus in the process of throwing himself off of a bridge. Mind you, this was no dinky wooden catwalk. If you 'Google Images' the phrase; Riva Road Bridge Image, three little maps will pop up. Next to those three little maps there will be a picture of a man fishing on a beach. The bridge in the background is the bridge next to the crab house. And that is the bridge that my friend did a double gainer back flip off of, while I sat and stuffed snow crab legs into my mouth, and washed them down with our fourth pitcher of Miller Lite. It was amazing. Thankfully, he wasn't hurt. He lost a shoe in the Severn River, but hey, it was very entertaining. The only bad thing was, he kind of smelled during the rest of our meal.

Once I spent an entire afternoon drinking my way through a snow storm with my friends. We decided that it would be *awesome* to tie an inner tube to the tailgate of my friends' truck. I was having a legendary time, until he took a corner too fast, and I went careening out of control, and yes, looming in the distance was a street lamp. But it wasn't a highway street lamp. Oh no. That would have been too easy. It was a library parking lot street lamp, which means it was surrounded by three feet of concrete that was about two feet high. Needless to say, I woke up with a pitch black bruise that stretched the length of my body. From my armpit to my thigh, to be exact. That bruise took longer to heal than the face of the previously mentioned heckler of pool-playing-cue-ball-tosser-guy. It was brutal. I'm trying to talk about other people's injuries, but I just have had so many. I once scraped off the entire lower portion of my back. Let me tell you, sliding across a gravelly paved surface after attempting to Ollie over an eight set, *after* two bottles of wine, with a hundred and ninety pound guy on top of you, will definitely strip away a few layers of the epidermis. Take my word for it. Also, don't get drunk and pass out in a place that is crawling with Brown Recluses'. No Bueno.

Bad decisions are an ala carte dish that is served with tequila. I swear I have never seen a list of side effects in the fine print on a bottle of booze. Usually, it just says what the ingredients and alcohol content are. The least favorite of all of my souvenirs? The DWI that I have under my belt. **That** will ruin about 16 months of your life. I don't know about you, but I will take losing a tooth any day!

Certain things are guaranteed to bring about injuries. Camping with alcohol. Boating with alcohol. Jet skiing with alcohol. Walking up a flight of stairs with alcohol. Skateboarding with alcohol. Horseback riding with alcohol. Driving a tractor with alcohol. Snowboarding with alcohol. You get the idea. Basically anything *fun*, mixed with booze, can be a dangerous situation. But none of the activities listed above, are more perilous than going to a *bar*, with alcohol. Strangely, out of all of the possibilities, *nothing* is more detrimental to your health than a bar fight. You will wake up and not be able to move, nor will you remember what happened last night. Then, looking in the mirror, (*after* you struggle to get out of bed for twenty minutes) you realize that, well, you won't be leaving the house for a few days. Hope your boss believes you when you call in and say you have a wicked case of Mono.

Chapter Twenty Seven
INFAMOUS FOR BEING STUPID

The Stereotypes

Every honest bartender will tell you upon asking. In fact, we are the undeclared **authority** on stereotyping. We have more inside information about race-related atrocities than any other profession on the planet. (Except maybe Hospital's, and the Unemployment Office.) Let us begin with the dance floor. If there is cheesy Electronica playing, you can bet that the three Asians in the room are going to be the first ones out on the dance floor. They will perform the New Age Break Dancing, while people like myself, just stand, point, and laugh, and somehow they think that they look really "dope". Funny, "dope" is the *exact* word I was going to use to describe it. What happened to actually *dancing*? Not to sound old, but, having a seizure on the dance floor is not what I consider fun. It's kind of like that home workout video that no one really wants to order, because it just looks like *way* too much work. While the Tae Bo video is being filmed on the dance floor, the Italian guy is fist pumping in the corner, with his ironed jeans (weird), gold chains, and fresh spray tan, scoping out the Snooki's of the room, beating up the beat, jumping around like a twelve year old at a Korn concert, and making a complete ass out of himself. All of this continues to happen, while the 'Brotha' is at the bar, ordering Ciroc, even though he doesn't know what it is or how much it costs, simply because P. Diddy, Puff Daddy, Sean Combs or whatever his name is at the moment, is on the flyer for Ciroc on the front door. Meanwhile, the unruly white guy, has his ear buds in, is swilling Jager, and starting a mosh pit, to the Pantera song that only *he* can hear. Enter the Mexican Mafia. The swarm has rolled in eight deep, scouted out a table near the bar, flashed gang signs at the surrounding members of utopia, sent out the re-con crew to rally some chicas together, and then their private party begins. Lots of Corona, Modelo Especial, and tequila. Of course, these guys don't ask for Patron, because that has somehow, some way become associated with the 'Hip Hop' genre. Hmmm. Maybe it's because every rapper and their mom has decided that Patron is the new Grey Goose. I remember back when Grey Goose blew up on the scene. Seems like a long time ago. There have been several since then. Courvoisier. Hennessy. Remy. What my favorite thing about all of these drinks is this. Sweetie. Let me explain Cognac to you. Cognac is an after dinner drink. Meaning, that you sip it out of a snifter, in a room full of gentlemen, who are smoking expensive cigars and wearing thousand dollar suits. You don't order it, mixed with cola, leaning across a bar whilst wearing sunglasses at *midnight*. The drinking crowd differs from bar to bar. At the golf course that I worked at, they only drank Ketel One and Tonic. At the 'Fine Dining' bar, it was all Pinot Grigio and Manhattan Martini's. At the sports bar, it was buckets of beer and shots of Tuaca. Again, with the stereotypes. Golfers do what they do. They have way too much money to conform. Football fans have two things on their minds. Winning, and getting fucked up. Asians want to chug Red Bull and see how many times they can spin around and how many different moves they can force their feet to do. Ever seen the beginning of *Footloose*?

Stereotyping is the politically incorrect way that we as members of society get away with insulting each other. As a matter of fact, the idea for this chapter hit me, about a week ago when I was on vacation with my friends in Vermont. We were in a secluded area, at the end of snowboarding season, and found ourselves in a dive bar surrounded by old white guys. I was standing around, waiting for one of the tourist-hating bartenders to actually pay attention to me, and one of the old white guys sitting at the bar looked at me, gave me a nonchalant once over, glanced back at the table packed with my friends, noticed what we were wearing, and said "Five snowboarders are in a car...who's driving? The cops." Ugh. I stood there for a moment, contemplating my response. Of course, this guy knew that we were a band of snowboarders, otherwise he might possibly have just said *hello*, or maybe asked me where I was from. *Instead*, he took the lower road, and was attempting to insult our little crew. It turns out, while he was fishing for cod, he caught a shark. It's ok. Getting kicked out of bars is not something I am unfamiliar with. While it may have been foreign territory, the retaliation was still spoken in the same language. I just did what I do, and then we were asked to leave. As we were escorted out though...I noticed that there were a few Asians on the dance floor. True story. Bringing me back to my original point. Stereotypes. No matter what walk of life you happen to hail from, whether it is Topeka or New York City- there is always going to be some inside joke about *other* people. This is what makes it so much fun. I'm sure that rappers make fun of punk rockers. I am sure that chefs make fun of caterers. I am sure that trash men make fun of recycling guys. I am sure that dry cleaners make fun of...*someone*... The fact that we as humans figure out a way to take jabs at *other* humans is not the problem. The problem with all of these stereotypes is that in some way...they are all *true*.

Chapter Twenty Eight
CHOOSE YOUR BOOZE

"You Say Potato…I Say Vodka…"

Figuring out what your choice alcohol turns out to be, is kind of like picking a mate. Sometimes, you have to kiss a few frogs before you find your prince. Of course, you need to experience *all* that each variety has to offer before committing to a partner, and naturally, not all of them are compatible with *you*. There are a few tell-tale signs that are guaranteed to prevent you from spending a lifetime making out with the toads, but you have to actually *pay attention* to the signs. Ignoring them, or chalking them up to 'just another drunken stupor' will land you right back where you started, and then you will remain the spinster, casually bouncing around, undecided and bored… until you die.

Tequila. *This* aqua vitae has a strange effect on some people. It makes them naked. Not everyone can handle the happy, and not everyone can figure out the flush that creeps into their cheeks, after tossing back a warming shot of the Agave based treat. Tequila is a party shot. When you are surrounded by friends, on a cold winter night, chilling in the hot tub, or sitting by a fire in the ski lodge, *then* it is okay pour a few rounds of shots. Other than that…you don't need to bust out the bottle of Quervo, because it will only end in sex. There are only a few people in this world that can handle swilling tequila out of a flask. And those people are scary.

Scotch is for rich people… and old guys. I can tell you fifteen different kinds of scotch, *but*, I have never tried it. Therefore, I have no words of wisdom to share with you about the way it tastes, the effect it might have on you, or what the aging process has to do with the flavor. Sorry…I'm not rich…or old.

Brandy. Anyone for cigars and boring discussion that drags on for hours on end about money and politics? Again, I am no authority on this distillation, nor would I like to be. I mean no disrespect to anyone who is a brandy fan…but, I am only *thirty*. I don't chew on cigars, and I don't really spend much time hanging out in the smoking room at mansions, especially with politicians.

Whiskey. The firewater can **also** have a strange effect on people. *Anger.* Perhaps it is one of the steps in the fermentation, perhaps it is just the body's natural reaction…who knows? My first alcohol experience was with Jack Daniels. With good reason, I have never touched it again. I punched my best friend, and I puked my guts out shortly thereafter. Whiskey is one of those things that force the people who drink it regularly to call it an "acquired taste". Personally, it's the *taste* that makes it so raunchy to me. The buzz can be okay (for a few minutes) if you can get past the nausea that occurs within seconds of it hitting your stomach. There are at least a dozen different types of whiskey, and if you are pursuing a relationship with this particular sauce, be sure to play the field. Maybe the Irish Mist or Jameson would be a better match than the Jack or Beam. If you are more of a 'mixed drink' rather than a 'shot' type of person, VO or Canadian Club might be a better choice, as I've heard it mixes better with cola than Crown Royal or Bushmills. Either way, your courtship with whiskey should be taken slowly. You never want to rush into claiming a partner…that's when you wind up in divorce court.

Rum. Oh the island treat and beloved broth of the pirates. I had a short love affair with rum myself, but it ended abruptly when I spent an evening making bad decisions on my balcony in the Bahamas. I tried to relight the fire once, and *only* once. Remember when I said I made a scene in Vegas? Bacardi Coco was to blame for my blasphemous behavior. There are over a hundred different flavors and forms of this delicious decoction. Rum creates an elevated lightheartedness that not a lot of other things in this world can provide...well, legally anyway. The average rum drinker usually opts for the 'lite' or 'spiced' rum. These are the ones that go down the smoothest, are easily mixable, and provide the coveted elation that has come to be expected of the rum buzz. There are others, however, that pack a little more punch. Goslings, Myers, Bacardi Select and a few others are the 'Dark' rums. Dark indeed. Ever caught a glimpse of someone that has had one too many Gosling's and coke and winds up naked in an a hammock? Do you know what a bed made out of rope does to even the sexiest of humans? Eew. In effort to avoid being the sloppy drunk that people are laughing at, you'd better do a little research in the comfortable confines of your own kitchen before venturing out in public and attempting to spend some quality time on the Dark side.

Gin. Other than actually *licking* a Pine Tree, nothing is closer to it than drinking gin. This Juniper extract was one of the original forms of intoxication. Dating back to the hooch running bootlegger days, gin is one of those liquors that you can*not* drink unless you are fully prepared for the repercussions. Gin drunk is like; Forget-my-name-don't-know-where-I-live-cant-remember-if-I-have-parents-or-what-their-names-are-might-as-well-handcuff-me-now-and-toss-me-Into-a-cell-to-avoid-any-charges-and-ensure-a-good-night's-*sleep* drunk... No one really *chooses* this lifemate, they just get stuck with it. Kind of like how the two ugliest kids in high school show up at prom together, get married have oodles of kids and stay together until the end of time. Must be somethin' in the Moonshine.

Liqueur. Sweet and savory. These appetizing potions are not only palatably pleasing, but low enough in alcohol content that if you so desired, you could sip them on ice until daybreak, *and* end the night without embarrassing incident. (Unless of course, we are talking about Sambuca.) Liqueurs' are meant to be after dinner compliments, daintily drank after a satisfying meal, when dessert was fantastic and wine just won't suffice. Frangelico, Chambord, Kahluah, Bailey's, Disaronno, these are the *lesser* of the evils. This list of suitors are the more appealing out of bachelors on the auctioning block. They won't get you into too much trouble, maybe a few quiet nights next to the fire, sharing in delightful moments together. Moving on to the more rebellious members of the liqueur cabinet. Goldschlager, Rumpelmintz, Aftershock, SoCo, Tuaca, Ouzo, Jager, (basically anything licorice, peppermint, or cinnamon flavored should be avoided) these are the boys that will lead you into temptation. You are no longer enjoying a blissful relationship, it is more like a domestic dispute.

Vodka. Feel like having the funniest night ever and then waking up in the bushes outside of the house that you grew up in, even though *no* one you know is currently living there? Maybe waking up in the backseat of your neighbors' car, simply because it is *nicer* than yours? How about being jerked out of a pleasant slumber to the sound of birds chirping...because there are *four* of them sitting on your face due to the fact that you slept on a fucking park bench with a bag of sunflower seeds in your pocket? These are the things that only can happen as a result of too much vodka. Forget the fancy Grey Goose, Belvedere, and Ciroc. They are overpriced and only famous because of the celebrities that *pretend* to drink them. I am a girl of simple tastes, and the playmate that I ended up choosing for a spouse was Smirnoff Orange. Perfect for sipping, shooting, mixing, or adding to a can of red bull, to make your trip to the zoo just a tad more interesting.

In easier times, with less emotional terrorism at stake, selecting someone with whom you wished to spend your time was probably a lot less technical. In this modern day, however, there are just way too many reckless conclusions being decided upon, which ultimately brings around a verdict that is somewhat unappealing for the ones on the market for a boozing buddy. Hopefully, this little guide through the basics will help those of you who have yet to find *The One*.

Now that you have the basic knowledge needed to peruse the alcohol dating scene, get out there and choose your booze. Don't say I didn't warn you, and please…drink responsibly.

Chapter Twenty Nine
THE REGULARS

You wanna go where everybody knows your name

Sigh Where does one begin the ride into regularity? Every bar has a few different sets of regulars. The daytime regulars are completely different than the 9:01 Club. The afternoon hour tends to bring in the older crowd, and they like to fuel up, and get the hell out of there before the heathens show up for the evening. In the biz, we sometimes refer to them as the 'daytime dwellers'. The ones who forego spending time in the sunshine and prefer to squander their afternoons hiding out in the formidable cave that is the bar. The one window in the far off corner doesn't allow in *too* many of the UV rays, therefore their old wrinkly skin isn't at risk. These guys file into the bar one by one, and as they enter, whistling the tune from *The Andy Griffith Show*, their bartender places their favorite beverages on the bar in front of them, without them having to utter a word. It is an unspoken rule, when you have reached regular status, you no longer need to order your drink. It is automatically waiting for you when you sit down in 'your' seat. The great thing about the afternoon delights' is that they don't require excessive time in the spotlight. Some pretzels, some beer, the occasional inappropriate joke. Smooth sailing. (Except for the one old curmudgeon that makes it a point to tell everyone, *every day* that he has been in a bad mood for twenty years.) Slowly, the sun begins to take its place in the western sky, and as predictably as they came in…they leave. Every resident has his estimated time of departure. It usually revolves around what time the wife is due home. So, again, one by one, they pay their tab and head home for the evening. Unfortunately, because they require so little attention, these are the ones that leave you a roll of quarters as a tip, because they have spent a few hundred bucks on Keno. *C'est la vie.* Take the good with the bad and prepare for the rest of your night. On to the next set of regulars. You can usually make the roster for the evening players depending on which nightly specials are being offered. If it is quarter draft night, you know which groups you will be seeing. The same goes for $8 steak night, two-for-one- Tuesdays, and every other crazy gimmick used to bring in the bawdy barrage of the younger versions of the daytime dwellers. What makes this job so enjoyable, is watching the goons that are all the lead character in their own low-budget movie. They are just as predictable as the day timers', but they tend to get way more intoxicated. Most of them don't have girlfriends (which is what brings them out in the first place) and if they do, they are just as guilty of alcoholism as their fellas'. For the most part they are fun, drunk, bitches, that spend their evenings pointing out what not to wear, by surveying the room and picking apart every other female on the premises. But occasionally, one of them gets a wild hair up her ass and then the Tri-Polar Disorder that she has been keeping a secret rears its ugly head. That, of course, is fucking hilarious, and we watch happily as she gets escorted to the door, flailing widly and yelling for her girlfriends' to grab her stuff and pay her tab. Sometimes her boyfriend followers her outside to take her drunk ass home, but then again, sometimes *he* is the reason for the fight in the first place so he stays behind, toasting with his friends and talking shit about her, even though everyone in the bar knows he is going to go to her house when he leaves. Sadly, this is not the first time that they have aired their dirty laundry at the bar. As a matter of fact...*I* tend to believe that this is their twisted version of foreplay. Moving on to the last set of regulars; that will pour in around midnight. We call these 'The Leftovers'. They have made all of their rounds, visiting all of the bars on their destination list, and this is the last stop before heading home for the night. Sometimes too incoherent to be served, they dutifully ask for water and settle onto a bar stool, whipping out their cell phone to perform what should be the simple task of calling a cab. Comically, this usually takes fifteen to twenty minutes of slurred exchanging of address information, but in the end, this responsible gesture is rewarded by their favorite bartender, when she slips him an end of the night shot on the sly. He then slips her a twenty, and all is right with the universe.

There are also those regulars that fall under the *that* guy category. Not that he is wearing a wife beater and sporting a blow-out...Just that he is that guy that everyone hates. Sometimes, there are *several* that guys' at any given bar. You know the ones who just *have* to tell every new bartender just how long they have been coming there. They insist on telling the same five stories over and over because they get so drunk that they can't remember who exactly they have told the story to. For some strange reason, they find it necessary to point out to the new girl that she is the new girl. Trust me, nothing in the world is harder than keeping a smile on your face, while some jack ass is pointing out the fact that you are indeed, *new*. I feel like screaming out, "Really? I'm so glad you are here to tell me that I am new here, because without your **profound** intellectual observations- I would totally not know that it's my first fucking day!" Captain Obvious, your table is now available... Have a seat dear drunk fellow, and try to make me feel a tad more uncomfortable than I already do... Jesus, maybe try a warm glass of *Shut the Hell up* and remember that you are the only one that thinks you are cool. The other regulars that make people hate them are the chair mongers. You know, the ones who refer to it as 'their' stool? The ones that will actually get pissed off if someone else is in 'their' seat. It amazes me, that just because you are at the bar *that* much, that you think that you have the right to claim a chair as your own. I had a guy at an old bar that would literally start arguments with other people if they were sitting in his seat. I feel like when these guys start acting like that, any bartender that witnesses it should be allowed to call him out in front of everyone by yelling "Hey, Turd...It's not *your* stool it's the *bars* stool! Maybe you should go home and put your kids to bed, maybe hang out with your wife and try to make up for eighteen years of being a douchebag. The other awesome idiots that I *must* make room for are the ones that used to work at the bar, and are either too old or too annoying to have kept their position. But, they always have to tell *everyone*, customers and new employees alike, that they used to work there. We get it buddy, you know everybody and you are aware of what the kitchen and the office look like on the inside. Whoopdee-fuckin-doo. But, I will say, without these guys to make fun of, we would start turning on each other a lot sooner. So, thanks for being a harassing henpeck, it's nice to have you there to hate, even if sometimes I dream about paying the bar back and his friends to nab you in the bathroom, and dunk your head in the toilet.

Being a regular is not an easy plight for anyone who wears the badge. It is almost like a job for them. God forbid something actually happens in *their* life that prevents them from showing up for a few days, maybe even a few weeks. As soon as he attempts to settle back into his daily routine, he is bombarded with questions about where he's been, what he has been doing, and what the hell took him so long to return. This continues for days at a time, as he has to listen to it from every bartender, and every other regular that has a staggered appearance at the bar. Poor guy. No one says they are sorry that his Grandma died, they instead berate him for not answering his phone for a week.

No matter which category that you fall into, being a Regular is an important role. We need you, we love you, we appreciate your business. While we might have altercations every now and again, these discrepancies in no way alter our affections for you. Each individual holds a special place in the history of the bar, contributing their own small personality traits that form the entirety of the *soul* of the joint. The tales that are told again and again, the family tree that continues to sprout new limbs, the legacy of the ones that pass on...these are the things that make this the most gratifying job on Earth. **Plus** the money... We don't want to leave *that* out. (It was getting a tad too sappy there for a moment...even for *me*).

Chapter Thirty
SPECIALTY DRINKS

"So...let me ask you...which one of these drinks takes the longest...
and is
*The biggest pain in the ass?...Cool...I'll have **that** one..."*

Anytime you see a group of girls walk into your bar...you are about to contemplate suicide. Let me assure you, they haven't even sat down before they are reaching for the specialty drink menu, and perusing the contents as stone faced and serious as if it were a plastic surgery waver that they were about to commit to. Frozen drinks, martinis, Bellini's, mojitos, crushes, margaritas... These are the most annoying and time consuming concoctions available, and of course...the most popular. I'd like to personally thank the creators of *Sex in the City* for bringing the martini back. Because, before *that **fucking*** show and *those **fucking*** women, exactly **what** were the whining, confused, lonely, and completely *desperate* women doing to piss off the bartenders in that great, big, thriving metropolis that we refer to as New York City? Dismally, this trend drifted outward... into *every* bar in America... and the bandwagon has become a damned stretched Hummer Limo that mated with a **BUS**, bringing into grasp the realization of the fact that this is no meager **trend**... oh no...*This* is a craze on crack, and it is here to stay.

The mania surrounding the martini is fine. Everybody likes to try something new. The problem with the 'specialty' martini is that, well, it isn't really 'special'... there are just eighteen different ways to alter a fucking French Martini. Add a star fruit as a garnish. Throw some Melon liqueur in with the sour mix. Freeze a raspberry into an ice cube, drop it into a martini glass filled with Apple Pucker, and float a little Blue Curacao on top...and *violas*... a new and exciting drink. Not so much. It tastes like shit, there is no alcohol in it, and it makes your breath smell like someone pooped in your mouth. **But**... if you toss a *blinking* plastic ice cube in it, rim the glass with electric pink sugar, and serve it whilst dangling upside down from a trapeze, naked, coated in bubbles, and swallow a flaming sword when you are finished pouring..**Well then**...Another round for the ladies, barkeep!

The **Mojito** on the other hand, is a somewhat newer fad. And I bet you a million mint sprigs that I can guess why this low-fat salad in a glass became the cat's pajamas. A couple of Americans took a holiday in Brazil, wandered into a cabana that doubled as a bar, and *fell in love*. The place was actually a hut made out of mud and straw, the dance floor consisted of yesterdays' hay, the joint had no walls, and the bar was a loosely constructed counter built out of driftwood and chicken wire...Yet, the ambience was *paradise*. There were a few hundred beautiful, tan, sweaty Brazilians, dancing sexily to the melodic horns and maracas, all swept up in an enchanted moment that only happens between two people in a foreign country, doing a foreign dance, drinking foreign drinks....And thus the birth of the Mojito in America. All because some *stupid* couple, trying to bag the magic that can only transcend while on exotic soil, attempts to bring some "culture" to the bar... Therefore enticing every *other* stupid couple in the room to tap into the "Ooooo, **that** looks new and interesting, let me hear the *story*..." source that resides in all *boring* people and the rest is history. Let me walk you through the process of this peculiar paragon. You drop three lime wedges into a pint glass. Add three to four mint leaves, sugar, a dash of elbow grease and a muddler. **After** spending forty-eight to one-hundred-and-fifty-six seconds smashing, twisting, and grinding those fucking limes into oblivion, you are left with a pulpy, herb smelling, green *mess*, which strangely, someone wants to put in their *mouth...* and then you add the simple syrup. Simple syrup is a concoction of water, sugar, and some sort of sticky liquid that ends up all over the service bar and turns into glue that is stronger than any other substance known to man. Add ice, rum, and club soda, give it a shake or two in a tumbler and there you have it. Unless you are a rum drinker, or a rabbit, this drink is not for you. You spend fifteen minutes trying to figure out why there is lettuce floating in your booze and if you are not careful, you wind up in conversation with the man of your dreams...only to find out later that you have a ton of green shit stuck in your teeth. Yeah... if I were you I would just skip over the Mojito menu... saves the bartenders from conspiring against you, and it bypasses the embarrassment you will suffer in the long run.

The Bellini. Ahhh the Bellini. This drink was designed *specifically* to be consumed in lavish and expensive brunch settings. A restaurant you could *never* afford and mid day parties that you would *never* be invited to. A bunch of yuppies dressed in their Sunday best, and waiters waltzing around in tuxedos, toting silver trays full of fancy French tidbits that you can neither pronounce nor bring yourself to sample. The Bellini is the decorative cocktail that frilly people like to sip on, to complete the image that they are portraying to the rest of the party. A Chrystal champagne flute brimming with Dom Perignon, with any number of elaborate fruit purees resting colorfully on the bottom of the glass. Most people prefer peach or strawberry, but you can get creative and toss just about any flavor inside of the bubbly. This is a wonderful and tasty treat if you are one of the fabulous people referenced above. If not...I implore you **not** to pretend to be. By ordering a Bellini, it is obvious that you are trying to send a message that you are a classy and elegant woman. Unfortunately, when you are in a sports bar, on dollar draft night...it kind of makes you come across as high maintenance and phony. Want to sip on Bellini's? Move to L.A... If you live in Podunk, stick to the dollar drafts...

What's next...? Ohhh *The Crushes*. It is impossible *not* to love them; they are, in fact amazingly delicious. However a bigger nuisance can*not* be invented. And I am not talking about the drink...I am talking about YOU. You know who you are. You are the ones who drink thirty of them every time you come to the bar. Just because you see a juicer sitting on the bar, does *not* mean that it is okay to order thirty of them! I am okay if you want one, maybe even two, which is fine (it's still a pain in the ass, but it can be overlooked if the *ahem* *compensation* is worth the trouble...) but any more than that and you are creeping into asshole territory. Don't get me wrong, I understand that it is my job to provide beverages for those who do not wish to stay home and create them for themselves, but, during a busy Friday happy hour, squeezing three hundred oranges for a two-dollar tip doesn't really light my fire, get it? That goes double for grapefruits, by the way. They are twice the size of oranges, and require muscles that no female is born with. There are at least ten different crushes on the menu at the tiki bar where I work, which means that there are at least ten different reasons I want to kill you by the end of the night. I encourage everyone to enjoy a crush every now and then, and after I encourage them to do that, I encourage them to pick a different drink to enjoy for the rest of the night. That is...If they want to continue to enjoy *breathing*...

Moving right along... The Frozen Drink. I believe I have touched on this subject numerous times already, but allow me to indulge in more detail. The Frozen Drink menu is something that is carefully thought up by managers brimming with excitement about the upcoming summer months. They attentively take all liqueurs into consideration; match them up miraculously with ice cream bases, strawberry syrup, pina colada mix, and the finished product winds up in a hurricane glass topped with whipped cream and a cherry. The problem with these brain freeze inducing by-products is that once a customer is served with one, the rest of the girls sitting around her suddenly decide that they absolutely *must* have the same thing. It just looks too scrumptious to pass up. Therefore, you are rinsing out your blender fifteen times, muttering under your breath, and finding it virtually impossible not to throw a cherry at someone's face. Heads up ladies, there is a reason that the strawberry daiquiri floating atop of the pina colada is named the 'pain in the ass'...

In summation, the specialty drink menu is a fun addition to any night out on the town, **but**, every patron should take into consideration their setting, the mood of their server, and the capacity of the establishment in which they are currently enjoying ice coldies. If there are more than fifty people asking for drinks, the partaker should then avoid ordering *anything* that might result in a menacing glare from the bartender. If the warning glance goes unnoticed by said partaker, and a *second* pain in the ass is requested, one should be aware of the ensuing intestinal disruption that will undoubtedly accompany their 'satisfying' beverage. Just sayin'.

Chapter Thirty One
COVER BANDS

"Oh my god, I LOVE this song...Oh Wait... "

I *used* to love this song... until I heard it *NINE HUNDRED TIMES*. There is one common denominator in the downfall of all good songs. Cover Bands. There are many great things to be said about those who possess a natural talent for music, and those who are awesome enough to channel that talent into something original and have the outcome be amazing. Amazing enough in fact, to have every single uninspired garage band decide that they would like to be as cool as you, by learning your moves, singing your songs, and achieve that rock star status by emulating your creations to a bar full of screaming drunks, that have had *just* enough alcohol, to not mind that the front man isn't the *real* Zack de la Rocha, and is instead a faux hawk sporting imposter, that happens to be equipped with a monster voice and enough energy to make them believe that they are actually at a Rage Against The Machine show. As a music lover, and somewhat of a connoisseur of certain bands and genres, it is downright painful to watch. While we, the staff, must present an excited and hospitable environment to the band, as they order their drinks during sound check, a few of us have our 'excitement' secretly diluted with mockery. Call me a snob if you will, but I would prefer a musician to show me his stuff. Wow me with his ability to take words and notes and combine the two into an audible treat. A chorus that gets stuck in my head for days at a time. A few lyrics that touch my mind in a way that is indescribable. Opening notes that render me incapable of paying attention to *anything* else for the three minutes that the song is playing. Instead, I have four bands a week playing the exact same songs as the ones who took the stage a week before. Actually, the set lists are *so* repetitive that we have designated *shots* to *songs*. I will explain. Within the first three notes of 'Laid' by *James*, I can count on the fact that when I turn around, one of the three other bartenders will be handing me a shot of Jager. It's the rules. Just like the moment we hear someone croon "*I got my first real six string…oh at the five and dime*" one or all of us reach for the tumbler to shake up a few team shots of vodka. It is so predictable. Whenever a lead singer thinks himself capable of spouting out a rendition of 'Evenflow' by Pearl Jam, I am stricken with the undesirable urge to explain to him that he is not old enough to remember the 90's grunge era, and he certainly isn't awesomely Eddie Vedder enough to confuse us with his jumbled opera-like vocals, *or* his passion for some kid named Jeremy…

The problem with most guys in cover bands is they aren't really aware of how silly they come across. Strangely, they are under the impression that they are *real* rock stars. I suppose it is the crowds fault. If one band plays at the same bar on the third Saturday of every month, and two hundred people show up for it, all stoked and ready for the 'show', the band gets more and more popular by word of mouth. Then the groupies start pounding vodka, dancing right in front of the stage, with their skirts pulled up and flinging their hair around like the chicks in old *Poison* videos. This also helps create the illusion that they are rocking out to a very famous group, and that any minute the roadies will begin throwing out backstage passes so they can all get naked and swim in tubs of champagne…

I sometimes have a hard time deciding which one is worse, the *band* or the chicks that throw themselves *at* the band…

Lately, I have noticed a new trend among cover bands. Most of them are all guy bands, with the occasional female lead singer. For some strange reason, the all *male* bands are learning and performing *chick* songs. Confused? Me too. At least I was the first time I heard the lyrics to a Lady Gaga song being belted out by the black guy with the Mohawk. At first I thought it was a joke...but much to my surprise, he sang the whole thing, actually *combined* it with **another** chick song, and the crowd loved it. Like a disease, this fad has infected almost every band in the area, and now, not only do I have to suffer through poorly constructed renditions of Johnny Cash tributes, I suddenly am trying to explain to my ears why they are being bombarded with craptastic music, and pleading with them to just tough it out for a few more hours, until we can climb behind the wheel of my beloved Wrangler together...and slip on a Sex Pistols CD for the long ride home.

Chapter Thirty Two
THE LINGO

The One Thing We All Have in Common

When you are at the office, I'm pretty sure no one ever says "We are 86 printer paper."

Likewise, I am confident when I assume that no one ever tells you that they need a FAX, *on the fly*, **NFL**." **HELP** probably means something *entirely* different, and "in the weeds" is most likely a terminology used for fishing trips in the Hamptons. We have a language that permits us to communicate quickly and without questions, allowing fewer words and more *time* to **haul ass**... which is necessary when you need to drop off a dying app to table nine, who we *forgot* to fire a second course for, while cold side is having a cow, sushi is backed up, frozen drinks are melting, and we have single handedly made the wait go from five to fifteen minutes for a turnover. Confused? You should be. We however, channeling our inner *Scrooge's*, must learn to speak the Dialect of Directors Past, or are forced to chug penalty shots of Yukon Jack out of storm pourers... Pay attention...I'm gonna talk *fast*...

Right behind, on your left, or *behind you slut!* is what we shout to avoid collision with another bartender. *Watch your head* means if you are kneeling down, the register drawer is open, and if you stand up, you will be knocked unconscious by a till cradling thousands of dollars. *Watch your coochie* or *Cup check!* Is what we shout when we are opening front loaded coolers to get a beer bottle... *On the fly* is code for '**fuck me! I forgot to ring it up and I need it** *right now-* **so throw that shit in the fryer...**' NFL means *no fucking lime*, and *buried* or *in the weeds* means you are *so* busy that you consider yelling 'fuck it', peeing in your pants and just *eating* a Marlboro Light because there is no fucking way that you are getting out of your hole for a good forty five minutes. It will be full on "*What'd'ya need, what'd'ya need, what'd'ya need* until the lights flicker. A *quick pour* is the metal jobby that sits on top of the liquor bottle, a *storm pourer* is that big plastic thing that the juice comes out of, the *gun* is where we get our soda, and the *well* is where we keep our ice. A *speed rack* is that knee busting metal thing that holds all of the booze, a *cover* is a person, a *camper* is a table that sits too long after they have paid the check, *no call no show* means an employee hasn't come in for their shift, and *early out* means that if it is slow, you get to sit down and start drinking. *Upsell* means you are supposed to suggest a pricier form of whatever they are ordering, a *walkout* is someone that dips on their tab, and *All Day* refers to how many of one item is on tickets that are hanging in the kitchen. FOH- front of house, BOH- back of house, MOD-is the manager on duty, GM- general manager, DICK at table twelve, self explanatory.

HELP. This can mean any number of things. One, of course is the signal for an extra set of ears and hands in your well, because shit has gotten so hectic, you (even though you hate to admit it) can't keep up. There are just too many different kinds of shots, shooters and bombs being ordered for your hands to work that quickly. I would personally like to grab the chick that asks for eight shots of Rumplemintz, two red headed sluts, three grape bombs, a cherry vodka and coke and a Singapore sling, and drag her across the bar, and tell her that she can have it for free if she can make it in less than three minutes. Oh, but then, when she says that they will all be paid for, *separately*, I will take her head and smash her face into the computer screen, and spend a peaceful night in jail, with no one asking me for *anything*. And that would be just fine with me.

The second thing that HELP could mean is; this guy is fucking freaking me out *please* wait on him even though he will wave you away, and insist on waiting until I am done waiting on the thirty other people that I have designated myself to, just to get away…
Not a creeper and not *that guy,* he is just weird. He only likes *you,* and he will wait all night just to watch you pour his beer. He's like Jack Nicholson in *As Good As it Gets*; he probably washes his hands a hundred times a day and avoids the cracks in the sidewalk. HELP could also mean, I really, really, *really* have to pee, so watch my corner, *or,* my cousin is shitfaced and starting a fight so I need to run outside. HELP is a universal one word SOS that we all understand, and no matter what the request, we all man up, and jump in when necessary.

In the Biz is pretty self explanatory. It refers to someone that also works in the service industry. Most places have a service industry night, trying to create a fun atmosphere for others to come and hang out in when they get done with their shift. Regrettably, when you bring together a few different groups of people from competing bars, it doesn't matter *how* great the 'Biz' discounts are, there is going to be tension. It's as intelligent as bringing East Coast and West Coast gangsters together, throwing some old school Italian Mobsters into the mix, and asking them to enjoy a quiet dinner with the highest members of the Klu Klux Klan and MS13. You would *think* that bartenders want to tip the hell out of other bartenders- I mean, I know *I* do, but alas, jealousy rears its ugly head and some people just can't let it go that our bar is more fun, our uniforms are cuter, and we make more money, so they act like two-year-olds and whine and complain and treat us like crap. They will be the first to stiff us, even after our computer gives them half off of their check, and sometimes, they even pull the old dine and dash, and then we have to pay out of pocket. It's ok, we know where they work. If they don't show up the next day with a fistful of cash, apologizing profusely for blacking out and forgetting to pay, they will wind up with a plastic bag full of fish guts zip tied to their engine. Do you know how long it takes to get rid of that smell?

Chapter Thirty Three
ETIQUETTE ACADEMY

...Nice Manners...Asshole...

If you have ever sat down at a bar, looked around, saw that the bartender was closing out a tab, picking up dishes and bidding farewell to another set of people, and somehow decided that waving her over and yelling out "Excuse me!" was an okay idea... you are an asshole. Trust me, the bartender saw you before you even walked in the building, and they are just trying to keep the good vibes that they were feeling from the last group going, even as they are walking out the door. Your turn is the next thing on their mind, and they are trying to have an equally as awesome of a conversation with *you*... But sadly, you just blew it. I think that you *others* have just grown so accustomed to people treating you like shit, that you don't fully understand that it is not necessary to demean other people once leaving your hostile environment. This is where I invite you to enroll in the Etiquette Academy. Everyone is guilty of being slightly disgusting on occasion. Picking a wedgie when we think no one is looking... sneezing suddenly without having time to cover our mouth and realizing that we just launched debris all over someone else's back...then being too embarrassed to tell them... using a fork to scratch our back...it happens. Being snide or looking down your nose at someone for whatever reason seems logical in your own mind, degrading a waitress, pinching a shooter girl on the ass, or deciding that it is okay to tell those around you that you once had sex with a stick shift in the parking lot of your high school... I implore you *not* to be one of these people. Stealing ashtrays, attempting to slip past the door guys at the end of the night with a beer in your purse, pounding on the cigarette machine, or car surfing in the parking lot... these are all topics in your lesson book. And of course, we must remember our manners...we wouldn't want grandma flipping over in her grave due to our unbelievably crass behavior...so PAY ATTENTION, CLASS.

For those of you that think you are still in school and need to raise your hand...I want to smack you in the face with a yard stick. I see you, and I am going to get to you- unless of course you are trying to hail me like a taxi cab. I like to refer to you as the **wavers**. You range in rudeness by how much of a spectacle you are making of yourselves with your waving. It is either a one-handed-smug-smiled-I'm-an-impatient-*fuck* wave (which is almost *always* followed by a judgmental glance while ordering) An I-used-to-compete-

In-the-special-Olympics-wave(which is accompanied by some form of grunting) or, my favorite; the double-armed-I-think-I-am-wearing-ear-muffs-and-landing-a-plane wave. I am hoping that you are signaling the Mother Ship, to come and cart you off back to your home planet...because this gesture makes no sense to me. Stop waving. I will be more than happy to get you a drink, as long as you admit beforehand, that you look like a royal jackass.

Which brings me to the next batch of should-be enlisters in my little school for the stupid... The Pointers. Sitting at the bar logged on to your laptop, with your Blackberry lined up next to your palm pilot, having a one-sided conversation with that wire that is hanging by your nipple, and then glancing at me, *pointing* at your half-full glass of whatever it is that you are drinking, and expecting me to know what the hell you are doing is flat out *obnoxious*. Maybe you could take into consideration that I wasn't the one that served you your **last** unappreciated beverage, and it wouldn't hurt to take four seconds to smile and say "Hey, I am a pompous jerkoff, and if you could find the time, maybe I could get another extra dry Beefeater on the rocks with one onion and two olives." Unless you are capable of peeling your eyes away from the computer screen that has become your life long enough to say this, go on pointing dude, and I will go on envisioning you as a retriever with a duck in your mouth.

Moving right along, the next to land on the Dean's list, are the ones who just can't seem to remember more than one drink at a time. If you are elected as the spokesman for the crew, then you better damn well have your shit together when it comes time to order. For those of you that *one* me to death, the Reaper holds a special place at the bar in Hell…just for you.

"Lemme get a Captain and coke." I make your drink. Squeeze your lime and smile.
"Five bucks."
"Oh, and a vodka and crandberry." I make your drink, a little less smiley this time.
"Ten bucks."
"Also, I need two Buds'." I get your beers, and begin to frown.
"Eighteen bucks."
"Gimme a Jack and ginger." I slam the glass in front of you. Are you getting the hint?
"Twenty four bucks."
"Also, I need a…" I then wait patiently; as you turn around for three minutes and begin laughing with the girl that won't have sex with you, while you waste my time and eight other people begin *waving…* here is a helpful hint from the Trixie School of *Not Getting Stabbed…* TELL ME YOUR ENTIRE ORDER OR I WILL SLIP THE DOOR GUYS A TWENTY TO TAKE YOU OUT BACK AND KICK THE SHIT OUT OF YOU BEHIND THE DUMPSTER…
As for the rest of the Oner's…You know who you are; the ones who pay your tab and then sit there for another hour asking for just *one* more drink…You suck too… How about you stop insisting that you are leaving and just drink your drinks for fucks' sake. We all know that you aren't going anywhere, and to top it off, in your head you already paid a bar tab, so the second one manages to slip your mind, and you walk out. So not only are we subjected to the irritation of

listening to you one us all evening, now we have to pay for your drinks out of our tip bucket. Jerk.

I mustn't forget the **whistlers,** because these morons are in a league of their own. I wonder exactly what in the blue *fuck* is going through their heads to make them think that it is even remotely okay to whistle at me to get my attention, and then laugh with their buddies like it was hilarious to treat me like shit. I like to walk over and serve the person *next* to the whistler, casually looking over at this offensive glutton and say "what…did you lose your dog or something?" Oh, and if you are one of the num-nuts with this guy, you are guilty by association, and I am ignoring you too. Get some new friends.

I believe that the '21 rule' should be a law passed by congress. You, upon turning twenty one, should be made to spend at least a year of your life working in the service industry. Maybe then you will know better than to ask for your check and tell me that you need to get home for bed, because you are one of those people with a "real job". I find that statement thoroughly ignorant. Is this my fake job…? Am I just pretending to go to work and bust my ass all night? Oh, and…you know I make more money than you, right?

Now, for the next semester in your quest for a diploma citing that you are *not* socially retarded. Stop Being Gross. Please recognize that you have bodily fluids and functions that no one else wants to be exposed to. Wanna blow your nose? Awesome…do it in the bathroom. Nobody wants to witness you playing 'Operation' in your snout, even if it is with a tissue. Do you like eating wings that are dripping with blue cheese? Cool. Chew with your mouth closed and wipe that shit off of your chin…Also, know that your lips, teeth, and tongue have been *on* said wing, and leaving your gnawed up bone on the bar insinuating that I am to discard it *for* you is **truly** disgusting, so put it on your plate, or have it removed from your colon, after I jam it up there with a pair of tongs from the kitchen. Do you enjoy making out with someone that you just met? Sensational. Please do it in a far off corner, where your drool, tongues and mouth bacteria are not in danger of coming into contact with me a*t all*.

People that work in offices or warehouses all day aren't really expected to touch four million things a night that other, more *unsanitary* folks have had in their possession, so I assume that they don't fully grasp the reason that the more experienced of us on the other side are so paranoid about germs. I had a boss once that made fun of me for keeping a tiny bottle of hand sanitizer next to the register, and for making a point of scrubbing up like I was preparing for surgery, every time I returned from the ladies room. I laughed at his jokes, and let him have his fun and then one day, I urged him to spend fifteen minutes in the men's room during happy hour. He honored my wish, sat in a stall pretending to be 'thinking', and listened as thirty or so guys came in and out, held their penis's in their hand, picked their nose, scratched their asses, and 'adjusted' their balls, and he said only two of them washed their hands before strolling out of the restroom and back to the bar where they were shaking hands and giving high fives to *other* polluted and unhygienic dirtbag's that are congregating.

The ladies room. Come on chicks, we are supposed to be the *clean* ones. There is some bio-hazard shit going on in the girls' bathroom at the end of the night. I have been in there during last call, 'hovering' carefully, and watched a well manicured hand reach down and pick old toilet paper up off of the floor to wipe, instead of just asking for some paper from a friendly co-drunker. For the 'ladies' that are either wearing heels that are too tall, pants that are too tight, or have had too many shots to balance correctly, pissing all over the toilet and floor is *unacceptable*. Then of course, there is the one that is so trashed that she has four friends surrounding her, taking up the whole damn bathroom, trying to keep her from falling over, while drying her tears for her and trying to wipe the snot off of her face. These are the things that your mother should have taught you not to do in public. Oh, and one more thing...No one wants to see your uterine waste floating in the toilet like a shark attack... so FLUSH.

Basically it is simple. Don't be gross or rude. Don't ask for separate checks. Don't come to the bar with pink eye or a cold sore. Refrain from talking with food in your mouth, participating in a game of tag-my-friend-with-a-used-condom, or trying to swipe your credit card in my cleavage, and everything should be just fine.

Chapter Thirty Four
D P C U

Don's Politically Correct University

A few months after I began writing this book, I changed my address. I also changed my hair from pink to purple, got a new tattoo, *and* I changed bars. Never in all of my years of pouring drinks for the 'others', have I ever come across a boss who equally points out all of the ways that I am awesome…and brutally *offensive.* No shocker to me, or anyone that knows me, I have a somewhat derogatory demeanor when it comes to my stage presence, but to Don, I have a laundry list of personality disorders and a slew of correctable habits. I think that I have become a *project* for him…He is determined almost, to make me *better.* The truth is I have been a mean and offensive asshole for *so* long, that it is hard for me to find my behavior inappropriate, accept of course, after I get fired for skipping over the bar and clocking someone in the face. Thankfully, I have yet to do anything so awful that he tossed me out on my ass, but then again, I have only worked for him for seven months.

Below is an archive of the different ways that I annoy Don on a daily basis, forcing him to summon all of the patience that one can muster, while still being stern *and* serious…but with a smile…even though it might be forced through gritted teeth…

Gum. I love gum. I have never really understood why it is *not* ok to chew gum. Gum makes my night go by quicker, and it is a way to keep my skull from splitting because *I* too, grit my teeth. I don't grit my teeth in my sleep, or when I am hanging out with my friends...I grit my teeth at *work* to prevent the index of obscenities from tumbling out of my mouth, when one too many people coax me into the 'bad place'. From what Don says, glimpsing a piece of rubber rolling around in my wide open trap is unacceptable. Therefore, he has deemed it illegal to enjoy a piece of Bubbilicious while running laps upon the mats. Immorally, I neglect this simple requirement, even though it is the easiest thing on Don's check list... **and,** to no avail, because he catches me red handed *every time*. *I* believe that he secretly has a gum-radar, which makes it impossible for one piece of the chewy to survive the length of the night. Every time that I am forced to spit out my peppermint wad, *Taps* is playing quietly in my head, and *then* I ponder a way to get the next piece, unnoticed...One day, I will figure out a way to chew gum without being spotted by the Wrigley Ranger...

Attention-Deficit-Hyperactivity-Disorder...More commonly known as ADHD... Unfortunately, I have lived with this malady since childhood, and now it has been imposed on Don, *and* his wife, Gretchen, not to mention the rest of the staff... recently I have discovered that Red Bull accelerates this madness, but I really, *really* like Red Bull. Sometimes I am aware of the ceaseless chatter that they are afflicted with, but, moreover, I am just *talking*. Talking all the time. Jumping, pacing, wandering, thinking. Trying to find a way to keep my mind occupied long enough to obstruct me from acceding to the lyrics or movies or books that are threatening to take over my brain, making me appear even stranger than I was a minute ago. Don has the distinct ability to entertain me long enough to get through my thought, and then he graciously changes the subject or sets off on an errand, rendering me incapable of finishing said thought, and then he casually points out all of the things I *could* be doing...instead of talking...

Swearing. Cussing. Cursing. However you label it, I am the authority on it. All of my life, -and I have had a pretty colorful existence- I have been pretty much incapable of expressing myself without being a tad vulgar along the way. It is just the way I talk. In my opinion, individual expressiveness is pivotal in finding out who you are as a person, even though regrettably, it becomes the reason your boss contemplates sending you to a reformatory. I tried to explain that the word *fuck* is merely an adjective, and in no way should it be considered any more abhorrent than *shazam!* Gravely, no one else seems to agree...

I find that I am a much more displeasing entity during the day, as I tend to forget that the sun is high in the sky, and most people are only interested in having a diet soda and a sandwich... and, crazily, not *one* of these stuffy suits want to listen to me belch or spout off profanity while scratching myself and swilling vodka...at *noon*...

The F bomb, to Don, is *not* fuck, however, it is Fag. Apparently, this is a way more insulting, repugnant word than fuck; which *sucks* because I say fag more than I say **Hello**... I don't call fags a fag, even though it shouldn't bother them because they are, in fact, fags...if someone called me a hetero I wouldn't get all faggy about it, I don't think I would be affected one way or another because I am, after all, a hetero. But that is beside the point. When I say fag, I mean *gay*. As in, stop being *gay* by watching that chick flick you **fag**, turn on the football game, and lets drink some beer and have some sex. It has nothing to do with sexual orientation or preference; quite frankly, I don't give a shit if you like it in the pooper. But, because I would like to at least *try* to be less opprobrious, I will refrain from using the F bomb so much...just for you Don.

Chapstik. I have a serious relationship with Chapstik. I cannot be without it for more than a few minutes, and if I am, I start to sweat. I panic. So it is no surprise that even when I am working, I am going to put on Chapstik every twelve minutes or so. According to Don, anytime your hands come within a few inches of your mouth, you need to wash them. Even though my hand is on the tube, other people might somehow misconstrue it as me jamming my fist in my mouth and drooling all over my fingers... And *no one* wants a drooly drink from a foul mouthed bartender... I don't see it, but Don says

I might as well stand behind the bar and pick my nose if I am going to put on Chapstik in front of people, and then neglect to wash my paws afterwards. Funny, I thought picking your nose sent an *entirely* different message, but hey, I have been wrong before…

Don hates repetitive noise. Fingernails tapping on *anything*, glasses clinking, pen caps being clicked on and off… all of these things drive him crazy. I do believe that I have already mentioned the fact that I like Red Bull, but I forgot to say how much I like iced tea, sugar, and coffee too. Seeing as how my parents have tried to get me to sit still or be quiet for more than a few seconds *my entire life* and have failed miserably at this feat, I suspect that no amount of encouragement from anybody including my boss, is going to bring about the sudden ability to exhibit self restraint. Most of the time I am unaware that I am even tapping or clicking or pacing or talking so even though it might get pointed out, in thirty seconds I am going to forget… as the three hundred ring circus in my head gets louder and more interesting- I tend to block out outside influences. It's not my fault. I blame genetics.

I feel like graduating from Don's Politically Correct University would take me a very, *very* long time. When I can hear I don't listen well, I have a small case of OCD, I am slightly neurotic, somewhat eccentric, annoyingly obnoxious and **super** loud. Sometimes I wonder how I have lasted in this business as long as I have. I suppose I have just been blessed with patient and pleasant co-workers that employ ear plugs as soon as I hit the front door. I believe I overheard Don say that when I am not wearing jeans to work, chewing gum, watching TV instead of waiting on customers, putting on Chapstik or calling someone a fag, I am a valuable commodity in his establishment, but again, I don't listen well. He very well could have said "What the fuck…was that jean wearing, TV watching *fag* just picking her fucking nose?"

Chapter Thirty Five
LAST CALL

*"If your girl looks better with the lights off…
close your eyes 'til you get outside"*

Closing time. Lights flickering. A mad scramble for the bar to get one last drink… before getting behind the wheel. The Deejay tossing out random insults to the sloppy's, that aren't appreciated by **anyone** quite like they are appreciated by the bartenders. The door guys breaking up the last minute fights that have erupted out front. The curiously drunk bartender that is wiping down *one* spot of the bar over and over again. This is the nightly routine that we put ourselves through, and trust me, this lighthearted description does nothing to paint an actual picture for you. The *That Guy*'s of the room trying to figure out where the after party is going to be, the too drunk chica's that have been left behind by the gang- bangers that they arrived with, The rookies running around looking for the walkouts. The end of the night for *you*, means that ours is about *halfway* over. We still get to clean up **your** mess, count our drawers, sort through the hundreds of one dollar bills, and plot the murder of our boss, who just appeared and yelled out the two most horrific words in the history of the world. ***Bar Clean***. The impromptu bar clean can be the demise of an owner, as we have been busting our asses all night, and the only thing getting us through that last half hour was the image of our bed, glowing in a light that was shining down from the Heavens, with sheer white draperies billowing around it…

calling us home. Meanwhile, this fucker has been either napping in the office, or boozing it up with his bevy of bimbo's, just waiting for the moment that he could pull out his trump card and drop the guillotine on our heads by announcing the fact that we were all going to spend the next three hours pulling every bottle out of the beer coolers, and climbing inside them to scrub them spotless. (We have already sent out the re-con squad to locate a muddy yet off the 'beaten path' spot suitable for his burial) To anyone in this business, a Bar Clean is the equivalent of having an air bubble injected into your main artery, by way of the most disgusting, disease ridden needle that you can *possibly* imagine, and being administered by Satan's Legion. You know you are fucked when you notice the bartenders that weren't even working tonight, showing up in their sweat pants at 3am. Two words for you, Mr. Owner... *Get in the fucking cooler and scrub it yourself, I'm going the fuck home.* Okay, so that was more like five words...but... you get the point. We would rather the bar clean be scheduled, posted a few weeks in advance, that way we know which night we can plan our suicide.

Last call brings out the hilarity that stews beneath the surface of our solemn faced Deejay. Where he has been playing it cool all night, *this* is his opportunity to make loud, drunken observations and awesomely funny declarations. I do that all night long and no one gives a shit. Why? Because I don't have a *microphone.* "The after party is at Dunkin Donuts!" He shouts. Suddenly, the doughnut shop is the late night hot spot. Why? Because the Deejay said so. "We don't care where ya go...but ya cant stay here.." is another one of my favorites. "Have a nice day, and drive safely." He boasts. (And then he pukes out the window of his truck, while swerving all over Route 1 on the way home) Meanwhile, if the owner has stumbled out *prior* to last call, and the ominous **Bar Clean** has been evaded, the once weary-eyed bartenders wondrously catch their third wind, are suddenly up for a game of beer pong, turning off their phones to avoid awkward calls from their significant others, and fighting over the remote for the jukebox.

Prerequisites for the issue of last call vary depending on which country you happen to currently reside in For instance, In New South Wales, Australia, there is no specified closing time. Bars can stay open for twenty four hours. (Although, in residential areas they can be forced to close at midnight.) New York, Hawaii, and Alaska have a 4 a.m. closing time, while The Dominican Republic requires that all bars be closed by 2 a.m. Some states allow the purchase of beer up until 5 a.m. While others cut off the thirsty members of the population by 6 p.m. on any given day of the week! Certain places ban alcohol altogether, calling themselves *Dry Counties*. And somehow they wonder why the surrounding areas have nicer condo's being built, fancier restaurants, and in some cases, ***paved roads***...

Even though I am a bartender, I believe that there should be a way to vote into order a standing law, citing that the standard closing time for each individual establishment be decided upon by the bar owners in every area under the sun. I wouldn't necessarily enjoy waiting on people until seven o' clock in the morning...but that's what shift availability and seniority are all about. I might be the one sitting *at* the bar, being grateful that I could still do a shot even though the sun was coming up. These of course, are the by-laws that every bartender pretends that they are capable of producing, that in some way we might be recognized for making a discernable difference in the world...for something *other* than getting you fucked up.

The end of the night is our *pre*-unwind time. (Our *real* unwind time will be enjoyed with a cold glass of vodka from the freezer, once we have navigated our way home, sometimes with the help of only one eye.) It is when we eat the leftovers in the fridge, chug bottles of water, and discuss the events of the evening. Trust me; we are making fun of you, *right now.* Cleaning, chatting, laughing, and listening to some much deserved tunes. Occasionally we are obligated to give each other a ride home, a place to crash or jam a finger down the throat of the too drunk waitress, who was discovered face down under a pool table. It is was makes us family.

Strangely, last call is the one moment that can be counted upon. That one last smile of appreciation that passes between the warriors, even after an I'm-going-to-punch- everyone-in-here-In-the-face-including-**you** kind of night. The feeling of serenity, of accomplishment, of *victory*, that passes through us cannot be bottled, cannot be sold, and cannot be bought. We have achieved the goal of every bartender in the world. ***Not walking out***. It is a fantastic moment when you are finished cleaning, when you are handed four hundred bucks, and when your keys slip into your ignition. Every time I shift my car into gear, I smile a smile that only ones from the other side can smile. It is a fabulous life we lead, and I get to do it all over again tomorrow.